CW00571709

ENDORSEMENTS

I feel very lucky to have had the opportunity to read your lovely, inspiring book. It stretched my brain and warmed my heart. I love the way you have it organized. It's uplifting, challenging, educational, practical, poignant, and intimate.

—Anne Grosboll
Educator (retired)

Dr. Al Bacchus explains—with depth and clarity—the nexus between body and soul, physiology and love. We are a unity of body, mind, and spirit. The practices set forth in this book can lead us all to vibrant health, better loving, and wholeness.

—Dr. Philip Bufithis
Professor of English, Emeritus, Shepherd University
(Author of the critical study *Norman Mailer*)

A must read! This book is clearly and well written. It seeks to promote the triple ideals of spiritual, physical, and mental wellbeing. The personal stories are humorous and good natured. Their inclusion brings the book to life and gives it that well-rounded feeling. A book to be enjoyed by academics and lay people alike. Highly recommended.

—Syletha Clark
Registered General Nurse (retired)
United Kingdom

You will find this book to be a treasure chest of thoroughly researched, integrated science. It is organized with unusual intellectual acuity to challenge your imagination and enable you to achieve wholeness in body, mind, and spirit. Dr. Bacchus tackles some lofty themes, interweaves his own experiences, and engages his readers in meaningful exercises. After reading, you will feel equipped and motivated to write your own story.

—Jeremiah O. Cox, Sr. MA (Comp. Sci.)
Erstwhile First Elder of Hanson Place Seventh-day Adventist Church in Brooklyn, NY, President of Hanson Place Church Support Corporation.

A fascinating book, an enjoyable read! Professor Bacchus relates incidents from his own life to teach valuable lessons on how to love more, how to attain high-level wellness, and how to be happy. Highly recommended.

—Thomas H. Benner
Attorney-at-law (retired), Martinsburg, WV

Dr. Bacchus has done a monumental job reintroducing the archetypes of maturity to a generation of young people that have grown up in a society of toxic masculinity. Coupled with his model for wellness, he offers a comprehensive guide for young men and women searching for a vision of wholeness.

—Raj A. G. Lewis, MA
Program Director, City Team Ministries, Chester, PA

I found your book *Love, Wellness, and Happiness*, difficult to put down because it seemed so integrative and easy to fit into my understanding and life. Loved and fascinated by what you did with the re-order of CS Lewis's love concepts. I especially love how this work just oozes from your life experiences, and so organically. It holds and hooks the reader as it is so much easier to make the ideas part of one's own life. I loved the way you kept challenging readers to write their own story and book. Awesome!

—Stephen Walwyn, MA
Marriage and Family Therapy, Silver Spring, MD

Dr. Bacchus has integrated principles of love, high-level wellness, and the keys to happiness into a practical framework for living your best life. I believe that this approach to fulfillment in life is useful for both Christians and non-Christians. As leader of health ministries at Rockville Full-Life Fellowship, Dr. Bacchus shared with our congregation some memorable exercises and inspiring applications that are found in these pages. I highly recommend *Love, Wellness, and Happiness.*

—Bill Neely, BD, MDiv
Former Pastor, Rockville Full-life Fellowship
Author, *The Gift of Criticism:*
Making the Most of Critical Communication
Founder/President of Getting Along Better, LLC,
a relationship consulting business

Dr. Bacchus provides a great framework for whole life reflection and healing. You will be stretched to examine your health, habits, behaviors, past, and spirituality as this book propels you toward writing your story to help others in their personal growth.

—Lyris Steuber, MS, LMFT
Licensed Marriage & Family Therapist, Orlando, FL

Reading this book will challenge you to learn, grow, and seek a version of yourself that is waiting to be brought to life. Dr. Bacchus's melding of science and faith serves as a balm for those seeking a comforting path in this often aggressive and controversial brave new world. Advising all to build upon a foundation of love is profoundly timely.

—Mary Ellen Rose, PhD
Comprehensive Health SME/consultant to the
Defense Health Agency
Foreign Service Institute, U.S. Dept. of State,
Washington D.C.

Now, more than ever, generations of young people around the world are disillusioned with society's incomplete vision of wellness and health. We are in desperate need of guidance and clarity from a sincere and trusted source. This book is what we have been waiting for. Dr. Bacchus has achieved something remarkable. He has recreated for his readers a clear and logical roadmap of the journey that led him toward true wellness and happiness. He has accomplished this by artfully weaving science, life experience, and the concept of love into an interactive adventure of self-discovery that others can learn from. In doing so, Dr. Bacchus challenges individuals to take part in their own introspective quest for wholeness. I highly recommend this book and know that countless others will benefit from his insights as I have.

—Josef Kruger, BA
Religion, Philosophy & Intercultural Communication

The most stunning statement in Dr. Bacchus's book is, "Wellness of the soul is more important than wellness of the body." Throughout the book this premise is dissected, scrutinized, magnified, and synthesized into a pragmatic approach, recognizing the importance of science but also the life-giving essence of faith. I believe his prayer and purpose for this book is summed up in 3rd John v2, "That you may prosper in all things and be in health, just as your soul prospers." As a physician, I am inspired to promote a "wellness epidemic," while continuing to promote a healing epidemic. Be sure to read Appendix 3!

—Glynn M Thompson, MD
Ob/Gyn Surgeon, Kaiser Permanente,
Gaithersburg, Maryland

The experiences and insights shared by Dr. Bacchus guide the reader on a path to understanding how to approach true and lasting wellness. This interactive guide helps to individualize the pursuit of whole-person happiness in a way that is eminently practical and applicable for this day-and-age. This book was a delight to read!

—Lynette A. Khan Parker, MD
Assistant Professor of Pathology, Ashton, Maryland

I highly recommend Dr. Bacchus's book *Love, Wellness, and Happiness*. It shows us that real life experiences help us see his very inspiring approach to wholeness through love. An awesome read! I'm sure I'll get even more from the second read when I make notes to weave my life story around my teaching philosophy for health and wellness.

—Bruce Peifer, MS
Associate Professor of Health and Exercise Science
Oakwood University, Huntsville, AL

Dr. Bacchus invites you to experience increased joy and wellness through a perusal of the wisdom he has gleaned from years of wellness coaching and teaching, a glimpse into his personal life story, and lessons learned through interesting applicable stories that draw you in. The read oozes with optimism and hope, and has an academic depth to it—I highly recommend it!

—Bruce Greenberg, MD
Fairview Health Associates, Summersville, WV

Love, Wellness, and Happiness

LOVE, WELLNESS, AND HAPPINESS

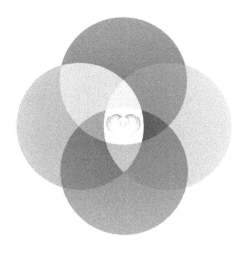

DISCOVER YOUR INNER WARRIOR,
MIRACLE-WORKER, LOVER, AND RULER

AL BACCHUS, PHD

Published by Author Academy Elite
PO Box 43, Powell, OH 43065
www.AuthorAcademyElite.com

Identifiers:
Library of Congress Control Number: 2021907523
ISBN: 978-1-64746-765-4 (paperback)
ISBN: 978-1-64746-766-1 (hardback)
ISBN: 978-1-64746-767-8 (ebook)

Available in paperback, hardback, and e-book.

All Scripture quotations are taken from Blue Letter Bible, a study compilation of several translations of the Bible available to the public at https://www.blueletterbible.org/.

Disclaimer: All information in this book is intended for educational and health promotion purposes, and does not replace the guidance of medical, legal, or other professionals.

To my wife, Carol

In celebration of the love that charted our
special adventure of 50 years so far.

CONTENTS

PART 3: YOUR BEST WARRIOR, MIRACLE-WORKER, LOVER, AND RULER

APPENDICES

FOREWORD

Humans were made to love and be loved. You may believe love developed through evolutionary forces as our strongest survival instinct. I believe this capacity of love is in our DNA and was intentionally grafted into our being when God created us "in His own image." Love is the foundation of happiness and a life well-lived. This conclusion is strongly supported in philosophy, psychology, religion, and sociology research.

In *Love, Wellness, and Happiness*, Dr. Bacchus refers us to the longest running research study in human development which started in 1940 and is still ongoing. After collecting data on the lives of a group of Harvard University students from graduation to death, the leader of the study came to these conclusions: *"Happiness is love, full stop."* And *"Happiness is only the cart; the horse is love."*

Building on the foundation of love, Dr. Bacchus explores our understanding of whole-person function. He then uses analogies from how the body works to make spiritual applications and recommendations for personal growth. This growth of body, mind, and spirit is the path to fulfillment and happiness. The summary framework is a 4 x 7 matrix that integrates love with physical, mental, psychosocial, and spiritual health. This is the definition of high-level wellness.

Dr. Bacchus demonstrates a deep passion for helping people to grow into a place of wholeness and healthy function as it relates to their full humanity. This book will raise your expectations for life and relationships. You were never created to be a victim and to merely survive in this existence. Dr. Bacchus creates a systematic process to guide us to a place of transformation and true fulfillment in life. Love, wellness, and happiness is what you were created for. Don't settle for anything less.

This book, *Love, Wellness, and Happiness,* is more than a quick read for enjoyment. It is a rich resource that can cultivate true happiness in your life. It is also packed with stories from real life experiences that may trigger you to review your life, and maybe write your book. I challenge you to follow Dr. Bacchus's personal growth cycle, and your life will be richer, fuller, and happier. In these pages which he calls, "my legacy piece," there are many practical tools to guide you through the process. Don't wait to get started in this book and establish your legacy.

Dr. Tony Colson, Pastor, ICON Church, Columbia, SC
Author, *Unlocking Your Divine DNA*
tony@tonycolson.com

A NOTE TO YOU—THE READER

I am a work in progress. I would like to share my story with you as I continue my search for meaning and savor happiness in life. I have struggled to honor my parents and yet follow my own interests in life. I have found it challenging to find a philosophy and strategy that work for me. I have come to the conclusion that my search will never actually end, but I can experience happiness in the process of searching. In fact, I have discovered that constant growth and discovery is key to a fulfilling life. It is important to discover a solid foundation on which to build.

You can benefit from this book by scanning through it. You may enjoy a superficial reading for the many stories and distilled wisdom. However, I believe you will benefit more if you do not simply read but interact by seriously reflecting on your life story. I will push you to reflect on your life, identify meaningful experiences, and consider writing your book.

I share not only my experience but resources and events that helped shape my experience. I hope they will be helpful for you as well. You have the option to passively read or become actively involved.

My story started on the island of St. Vincent in the Caribbean. My parents were third generation descendants of emigrants from India who came as indentured laborers. We were a small minority on the island with a population of around 100,000.

I was blessed to have loving (including tough love via the strap), hard-working parents. They placed a high value on education and encouraged all ten of their children to go as far as possible. After high school on the island, my education was all in the USA.

My journey has not always been smooth, and definitely not some fast track to success. But as I look back at my humble beginnings, I could never have dreamed I would be where I am today. My journey has not been easy, but the failures and successes have all been beneficial; anything worthwhile takes effort.

I hope the time and effort you invest in this book will enrich your life and help you to experience a life filled with love, high-level wellness, and true happiness.

One of the biggest, life changing moments in my life that shifted both my philosophy and career direction, occurred in Takoma Park, Maryland. That story starts the introduction to my legacy piece as I approach my seventy-fifth birthday.

I hope you take the more demanding path in exploring the contents of this book. And I hope it inspires you to write your story.

—Al

INTRODUCTION

In 1981, home mortgage interest rates in the USA reached a staggering 16%. Our house in Charlottesville, Virginia, was on the market. I had taken a job in Takoma Park, Maryland, and decided to move before the house sold. As encouragement to accept the job, I was offered the opportunity to purchase a home in Maryland as a co-owner with my employer. Without having a contract on the house in Virginia, I fell for the buying trap and lived to regret it.

The winter of 1982 was severely cold. The pipes in the crawlspace of the Maryland house froze, causing pipes in the master bathroom to burst. I called in *Johnny-Be-Quick,* the emergency plumbers. As they tore out the busted pipes, I was beating myself up for a poor decision. My anger boiled over into a tirade about being deceived on the condition of the house because I had left the inspection up to the co-owner.

I had worked myself up close to the heart attack stage of the stress reaction when the TV program was interrupted with a news flash. Air Florida Flight # 90 had crashed into the frozen Potomac River on take-off from Reagan National Airport. The live videos showed passengers struggling to stay alive in the frigid, ice-crusted water. There were dramatic rescues, but 78 lives were lost.[1]

Suddenly, my frozen pipes paled into insignificance. I calmed down and prayed for the victims and survivors of the plane crash.

However, I reserved some choice words for a meeting with my employer.

Long story short, I walked off the job. The University of Maryland Department of Health Education took me in and nurtured my new interest in health, stress management, nutrition and health education program planning. A teaching assistantship kept bread on the table while I searched for a full-time job.

In some heart-to-heart conversations with Dr. John Burt, chairman of the department, he encouraged me to create a course for the adult education program. The result was teaching "Personal Wellness & Self-Realization (HLTH 498-P)" for 15 years, and publishing a book, *Personal Wellness: How to Go the Distance*, with my wife as co-author.[2]

Those were the precipitating events that prepared me to blend life lessons with the wellness model developed in the course, and being ready to write *Love, Wellness, and Happiness*.

In the course "Personal Wellness & Self-Realization," every student had to create a notebook as if they were writing a book. At the end of the semester, all the books would be on display, and each author had three minutes to show their cover and tell the highlights of their work. This practice followed into my teaching the courses "Healthier Living" and "Christ-Centered Wellness" at Washington Adventist University.

As you take this journey with me, you will review your life, beliefs, and values. You will interpret precipitating events and their effects and apply wellness strategies as you determine their necessity in your life. You will purposefully cultivate positive qualities and seek to eradicate the negatives—we all have them. You will see that love is the foundation of happiness. This will serve as encouragement and motivation to strive for the high-level wellness path of growth, which will take you to the conclusion that happiness is not the goal to pursue—it is the natural byproduct of a life well-lived. And you will be ready to write your book.

The title of this book highlights the key concepts within. Love is the foundation of the framework and of human life. Wellness refers to optimum health in all aspects of function. The keys to wellness of the body are applicable, by analogy, to wellness of the soul. Happiness is defined in the classical terms of the outcome—a summary conclusion on the sense of satisfaction with who you are, what you are doing, and where you are going.

The Warrior, Miracle-Worker, Lover, and Ruler symbols are based on the concept of Carl Jung in what he termed "the archetypes."[3] An archetype is a symbolic character that embodies a related set of qualities. I use this concept to concentrate on the positive qualities. In wellness education and wellness coaching, I emphasize growth in positive qualities. The growing field of positive psychology promotes this approach in therapy as well. I first studied the archetypes through the research published by Robert Moore and Douglas Gillette in their 1990 book, *King, Warrior, Magician, Lover: Rediscovering the Archetypes of the Mature Masculine.*[4]

Throughout this book, I share principles and practices applicable to all belief systems. The content was shaped originally for an adult education course developed for the University of Maryland University College (currently the University of Maryland Global Campus). As such, the content and discussions accommodated all religions and philosophical perspectives. The original publication from that content was a more academic textbook.

Love, Wellness, and Happiness seeks to bring a revised, updated version of the original concepts to readers in a less academic presentation, better suited for personal study and application to personal growth. At the same time, there are lots of additional resources given in the Notes (Appendix 5) to make this book useful as the foundation for an adult study group (social or religious), an adult education course, a continuing education seminar series, or even a high-school course on happiness. I will be using it as part of the training curriculum that results in the qualification "Certified Wellness Coach."

In Part 1 of this book, I'll present an illustration, give you a chance to write what you see in the picture, then talk about the intent behind it. If you don't have the time or energy to probe your thinking, just move on to the explanation. I hope this serves you well in stimulating your thinking on the topic. In Chapter 13, I encourage you to write your book.

To be true to my deeply held religious beliefs, and to be authentic with my readers and clients, I show how the book's major themes connect to the core beliefs of Christianity.

This book's intended audience are adults who enjoy digging deeper into understanding themselves and acting on what they learn. I have had more women than men in my courses, and I expect more women than men will read this book. Surveys show women are leading the adventure of using alternative therapies and optimizing wellness and happiness.[5]

My best wishes to you as you start this journey with me.

PART 1

THE SELF, LOVE, WELLNESS, AND HAPPINESS

As one's sleep-smothered consciousness wrestles with a nightmare in its efforts to awake, so the submerged self struggles to free itself from its complexities and come out into the open.

—Rabindranath Tagore
(Nobel Prize for Literature, 1913)

1

SELF, LOVE, AND OTHERS

Amor vincit omnia (Love conquers all things).

—Virgil, Eclogue X

On a flight from Michigan to visit my parents in St. Vincent, I had a lay-over in Barbados. I walked into the gift shop at the airport and the first book that caught my attention was *The Four Loves* by C. S. Lewis.[1]

I had brought my human physiology textbook and notes on this trip as I prepared to take the doctoral comprehensive exams when I got back to Michigan State University. Reading *The Four Loves* captured my full attention on the flight back—a welcome rest from memorizing details of human physiology. The idea that the four loves defined four dimensions of human function stuck with me. My physiology material seemed neatly organized into seven subject areas: homeostasis, nutrition, stress adaptation, work/exercise, rest, growth, and reproduction. It clicked that here was a 4 x 7 matrix for organizing and evaluating human functions. The idea got filed for possibly later use.

Seven years later, my cup of joy overflowed when the chairman of the Department of Health Education at the University of Maryland said to me, "Create a course to be offered in the adult education program, name it what you want, teach what you want, and teach it how you want." One of the greatest thrills in academia is to have the freedom to create a new course.

After presenting several course titles and a completed syllabus, the departmental secretary chose "Personal Wellness & Self-Realization" to go on the course listings. (This might have been the very first college level course with *wellness* in its title. "Wellness" was not in the mainstream health education terminology in 1984.)

As I began planning the course, the four by seven matrix jumped to the forefront of my thinking. I discussed the project with my wife, and we decided we should teach the course together. We focused our course goals on the challenges we faced as young parents and chose a discussion format instead of a lecture format.

The Socratic method, which leads students to think critically and ask more questions, is a major pillar of adult education.[2] We decided to illustrate concepts that could be synthesized and used them to start discussions. With Harvard Graphics 1.0, the only computerized drawing software available then, we drew and took the illustrations to class to kick off discussions.

Here, I'll follow that format where applicable and trigger your thinking with an illustration before discussing the topic, and along the way I will encourage you to write your own book. That's what I did in "Personal Wellness & Self-Realization" at the University of Maryland University College and in "Healthier Living" at Columbia Union College. I fully believe every life has a unique story worth knowing and reading about. Only you know the details of your story, and only you can tell that story.

We found a lot of self-administered therapy in discussing and writing about our lives, and we enjoy stimulating others to examine their lives and write their stories.

So, here goes!

The illustration below seeks to clarify our understanding of who a person is. Examine the illustration and write what comes to your mind. There is no right or wrong answer.

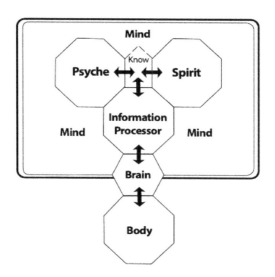

Write a few ideas you see in the diagram above:

_____

_____

_____

_____

_____

Let's review the ideas we tried to capture in the diagram.

o A person is a composite of a body and a mind.
o The brain is part of the body and brain function gives rise to the mind.
o The mind is bigger and more important than the body.
o There is two-way communication between the body and the mind.
o One major function of the mind is to process information.
o Knowledge is the result of information processing.
o The mind generates knowledge, consciousness, and evaluation of self, resulting in establishing what has been termed the psyche.
o The mind generates beliefs, values, understandings, and suppositions about ideas that transcend this world and the human body. We term the results of these functions "spirit," and refer to these things as spiritual.
o The mind can synthesize information and knowledge from the information processor, psyche, and spirit, generating new ideas and designs.
o A person's total knowledge and understanding is a constant flow among the information processor, psyche, and spirit.
o The body supports the mind. When the body dies, the mind dies.

WE THINK IN TERMS OF A WHOLE PERSON INTEGRATING ALL FUNCTIONS TO LIVE THE BEST LIFE POSSIBLE.

We no longer think of body and mind separately. We think in terms of a whole person integrating all functions to live the best life possible.

This composite, integrated person is built to love and to be loved. That is the most fundamental conclusion I can draw after my many years of studying human physiology, psychology, spirituality, health, and wellness. The four Greek words for love provide a much deeper understanding of love than the single English word, "love."

After reading C. S. Lewis's *The Four Loves*, I came away with the sense that love is the foundation, the underpinnings of our personhood. The types of love as presented by Lewis are:

o Storge (STOR-gay, with a hard 'g') is affection, love ruled by decisions.
o Eros (EH-rus) is sensual love connected to biology, sexual drives, and sensory pleasures.
o Philia (FIL-ee-ah) refers to friendship with deeply felt caring as in the term Philadelphia, for brotherly love.
o Agape (ah-GAH-pay), the highest form of love, means unconditional love and acceptance that transcends human love. This is the ideal love, and in religion, God's love.

Lewis felt that storge love is closer to what animals may feel. I disagreed on this point and use eros as the love more deeply anchored in the biology of the body, more common to the animal reproductive drives, and more dependent on sensory inputs into the brain. With this reorder, I created this visual for discussion:

Physiologic	Mental	Psychosocial	Spiritual
Eros	Storge	Philia	Agape

If this organization of love and human function makes sense to you, you may want to adopt it for organizing some aspect of your book. Make notes here of any ideas that come to mind.

_____

_____

_____

With the four dimensions of love aligned with the four dimensions of human function, let's examine what we may learn about love from the dynamic processes of our physiology. As I said before, when we study the details of human function, we can organize them into seven dynamic processes:

o Homeostasis—the maintenance of balance based on chemistry and nervous mechanisms
o Nutrition—supplying necessary chemicals to fuel the metabolic pathways
o Stress Adaptation—nervous and hormonal mechanisms to prevent or reduce the negative effects of stress
o Work/exercise—the use of energy to perform internal work, and work on the environment
o Rest—periods of cessation from work to allow recovery and repair
o Growth—stages of development from a single cell, and stages from birth to old age and death
o Reproduction—creating offspring for continuation of the species

These are the life-giving, life-sustaining processes of our biology.

Suppose we examine love through the lens of these dynamic processes. If love is the foundation, then all functions rest on love. We may ask these questions:

1. What is the balance to be maintained?
2. What is food for love?
3. How does love adapt to stressors?
4. What is the work of love?
5. Does love ever need rest?
6. What are the growth stages of love?
7. How does love reproduce?

Here's the visual for these relationships:

	Balance				
	Nutrition				
Dynamic	Stress Adaptation				
Processes of	Work				
	Rest				
Function →	Growth				
	Reproduction				
Dimensions of Function →		Physiologic	Mental	Psychosocial	Spiritual
Love →		Eros	Storge	Philia	Agape

It seems we have a lot to say about love. This matrix gives us 28 key ideas to pursue via seven leading questions. My answers may not be your answers. I will share with you some of my answers as you promise to explore yours.

We will discuss the table above in Chapter 2. We'll talk about all the applications of love in the integrated person. We'll share love stories, how we interpret life events where love is, and where it is not. We'll explore what shapes our capacity to love and be loved. I'll encourage you to write your love stories in preparation for publishing your book. And I'll promise you this:

When you are ready to write your book, I will share my successful book proposal with you to help you get started on the publication process. I believe you have a story that should be told to help someone else on this path of a happy life. If you feel the slightest inspiration to write, let nothing hold you back.

Make a few notes here of ideas that have come to mind for your book. (*If you can improve on any of my illustrations, feel free to adapt them to your material. I have full rights and will be generous with permissions. Just ask first.)*

_____

_____

_____

_____

Before we move on to chapter 2, there's one more thinking exercise to stimulate your self-exploration.

Universal Relationships of a Person

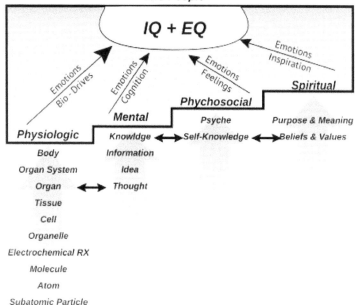

Cosmos
Galaxy
Solar System
World
Community & Nation
Family, Work, Friends
Two People

IQ + EQ

Emotions
Inspiration

Emotions
Bio - Drives

Emotions
Cognition

Emotions
Feelings

Spiritual

Phychosocial

Mental

Psyche

Purpose & Meaning

Physiologic

Knowldge ⟷ Self-Knowledge ⟷ Beliefs & Values

Body

Information

Organ System

Idea

Organ ⟷ Thought

Tissue

Cell

Organelle

Electrochemical RX

Molecule

Atom

Subatomic Particle

Look at the diagram above and write down anything that comes to mind. There is no right or wrong answer. (Suggestion: start in the lower left corner at "Sub-atomic particle," then follow to the top "Cosmos.")

Write what you see here:

_____

_____

_____

_____

_____

_____

_____

_____

_____

_____

_____

_____

Here's what we intended in this illustration:

o The four dimensions of function (physiologic, mental, psychosocial, and spiritual) are arranged in a staircase relationship with spiritual function as the highest.

o From sub-atomic particles to body, you see increasing complexity.

o At the organ level of brain, the ability to process information and establish intelligence is the first level that separates humans from other members of the animal kingdom.

o As the information processor handles conscious and subconscious knowledge, we form a body of self-knowledge which is the psyche.

o As the information processor integrates what we are taught and extract from life experiences, we establish beliefs and values that lead to asking questions about existence, purpose, and meaning. Questions such as: What are we doing here on Earth? Is this all there is? What's next? These are questions of a spiritual nature.

o Each dimension of function contributes its special drives which integrate into the emotions. Emotions percolate to the level of consciousness and find expression in behaviors according to individual patterns.

o A functional person is a composite of information processing intelligence (IQ), and emotional intelligence (EQ).

o Every individual must interact with others. The first interaction is with a mother.

o Life experience is made up of relationships.

o The most distant relationship is projected to the farthest reaches of the cosmos. Religion seeks to make this relationship the closest.

So love, in its four dimensions, is the foundation of human function. Love integrates the whole person. Whole-Person wellness can be defined as: "the product of the effort and attitudes we bring to the process of living the best life possible."[3] That best life possible has love at its foundation.

NOTES FOR YOUR BOOK

_____

_____

_____

_____

_____

_____

_____

_____

_____

_____

_____

_____

_____

_____

_____

_____

_____

2
WHOLE-PERSON LOVE

Where there is love, there is life.

—Mahatma Gandhi

Let's begin with the questions we posed about love:

1. What is the balance to be maintained?
2. What is food for love?
3. How does love adapt to stressors?
4. What is the work required of love?
5. Does love ever need rest?
6. What are the growth stages of love?
7. How does love reproduce?

Look again at the relationships we established in Chapter 1 about a functional person and love.

		Physiologic	Mental	Psychosocial	Spiritual
Dynamic Processes of Function →	Balance				
	Nutrition				
	Stress Adaptation				
	Work				
	Rest				
	Growth				
	Reproduction				
Dimensions of Function →		Physiologic	Mental	Psychosocial	Spiritual
Love →		Eros	Storge	Philia	Agape

The 28 empty cells above are there to draw out your thinking, and your stories. Stories I will share include: *Conversation with a Sex Addict; My First Girlfriend; Forgiveness from My Second Girlfriend 55 Years Later; Forgiveness for a Scar on His Leg;* and, *A Religious Ritual that Restored a Relationship.*

What thoughts and/or stories come to your mind? Pick an empty block, note the label for the row and the column, and see what thoughts or questions come to mind. For example, in the block where "reproduction" and "mental (storge)" meet, what thoughts about mental reproduction come to mind?

Make notes here.

_____

_____

_____

Let's examine those empty blocks beginning with reproduction in the physiologic (eros) dimension.

EROS: LOVE IN THE PHYSIOLOGIC DIMENSION—THE EROTIC CLIMAX

REPRODUCTION

Eros is based on body chemistry, electrical impulses, hormones, and the sensations that rise to the level of awareness in the brain. Then, the ultimate expression of eros is a burst of brain output that integrates all the input. This coordinated discharge of electricity and euphoria results in what we call the sexual climax. It should be obvious that our word "erotic" is derived from the root word "eros."

The complete relaxation and euphoria are coordinated by chemicals such as dopamine, norepinephrine, serotonin, oxytocin, and endorphins. The brain is the real sex organ. The sexual climax triggers a reset of baseline activity in the brain. It promotes sleep and increases the bonding, caring, and valuing of the sexual partners.

The primary biological objective of the sexual climax is to deposit a sperm cell on its way to meet its partner, the ovum. This union starts the reproduction of offspring to continue the species.

GROWTH

To understand eros better, we need to ask the next question: what are the stages of growth? Consider the sex drive from the responses of the teenage, male brain. That brain is more focused on how it can receive stimulating input, than how it may contribute to the source of that stimulation.

Then, eros grows as the brain ages, into seeking ways to create pleasure for the partner. The flames of eros simmer down to the brightly glowing heat of middle age. This is followed by the warmth of aging as eros wanes. This waning does not mean love weakens. Other aspects of love carry the same value and worth into old age.

This pattern of the growth of eros varies for each pair of love partners. Modern medicine then creates miracle drugs such as Viagra and Cialis, and greater individual variations happen. Men in their seventies behave like teenagers again—so I've heard!

Once upon a time, the teenage female brain was content with providing the stimulation the male brain sought. Now, that female brain has evolved to equality in giving and seeking the pleasures of eros.[1]

The pattern of increasing and decreasing sexual desire varies with hormonal changes. The most dramatic change is at menopause.

Yes, there is a female Viagra. The FDA has approved two drugs—Addyi and Vyleesi—to help women with hypoactive sexual desire disorder.[2]

But eros is not just about sex. Every sensory system contributes to the experience of pleasure based in eros. Think of sight—beautiful scenery and art. To a male brain so coded, the female body is the most beautiful scenery and art.

Hearing, smell, and touch are sensory inputs into the brain that enhance sexual pleasure. They have their own pleasure input independent of sex. Growth of eros calls for active experiences that produce pleasurable impulses into the brain. All the senses bring non-sexual pleasurable input to the brain. And all the senses contribute to optimum sex. The quality of both sets of input can be affected by the aging of the senses.

REST

Does eros need rest? Well, optimum sex involves rest between bouts of vigor! At least that is a safe recommendation for reducing the incidents of heart attacks during sex. But abstinence from sex—voluntary or involuntary—is a type of rest. Some couples use abstinence as a type of fast during a spiritual or religious exercise.[3]

WORK

The physical work of the sex act is designed to achieve sexual climax. Sex is recommended as a form of exercise. As exercise, frequency, intensity, and duration are factors to consider.

Part of the growth in eros is to arrive at what works. Work in eros may also relate to effort to achieve optimum sex. My definition of optimum sex is when both partners have a running, friendly, teasing, playful debate about who enjoys it the most.

Work, rest, and growth are intertwined. You can overwork in the act—older men have been known to have heart attacks during sex.[4]

STRESS ADAPTATION

Eros can produce stress when partners are not compatible. There are many sides to incompatibility. In all my teaching and coaching health and wellness, I've encountered only one case of physical fit incompatibility—he was too big, and she was too small.

Eros is a great stress reducer and the best sleeping pill ever. A major aim of stress reduction is the complete relaxation of all muscles. When this is accompanied by a euphoric storm that reaches every nerve, muscle, and joint in the body, stress reduction is enhanced. The erotic climax does that.

NUTRITION

In William Shakespeare's play *Twelfth Night,* Duke Orsino proclaims, "If music be the food of love, play on." But he is asking for that to give himself permission to overeat and kill his appetite![5]

Music, poetry, romantic novels, movies, sentimental murmurings ("I love you"), tender attention, and jovial teasing are all food for eros. The "love songs" of your teenage years are hard to forget. Enjoying these oldies together as you age is good food.

And memories are good food. Memories of the first time, the unusual places, the romantic trips, the experimental positions, the first night of the honeymoon, and the savoring of the "empty nest syndrome" are all good nutrition for eros. Of course, some memories may be painful, but there are lessons on what love needs to thrive, even in painful memories.

> BALANCE IN EROS INVOLVES THE EFFORT TO OBSERVE BOUNDARIES.

HOMEOSTASIS—BALANCE

The idea of balance has a lot to do with eros. Even though reproduction is the highest biological goal of all living things, eros has to fit into but not dominate life. Eros for sheer pleasure helps to bond partners together. Each brain awards value and worth to the source of the euphoria of the erotic climax. Balance in frequency, intensity, and duration are specific to each couple and takes effort to achieve.

Balance in eros involves the effort to observe boundaries. Boundaries include sex with children and siblings or with other people's partners. If boundaries and balance are observed, there will be no rape or forced sex in or out of marriage, no incest, no sexual harassment, and fewer instances of painful sex.[6]

****

STORY: CONVERSATION
WITH A SEX ADDICT

One of the rules of self-disclosure we follow in all our seminars is: carefully consider before revealing private information or personal behavior if it would make anyone uncomfortable. In this case, the individual started by saying her weekend had been "one magnificent pleasure high." She had a male lover visit one day and a female lover the next. At that point, the group stopped her from giving further details.

However, she had some interesting insights to share, and asked to talk with me privately. She gave me permission to use her story. Here is the story, reconstructed and paraphrased with some details changed to protect privacy. I have no reason to think it was a concocted story, and no reason to verify it. I accept it as truth. See what you think.

"It seems in my adult life I have developed a stronger and stronger addiction to sex. In my mid-thirties, I feel driven to make love as often as I have the opportunity—two, three, even five times a day. In the process, I have had several lovers of both genders, with some relationships lasting from a few months to several years, and often more than one at the same time.

"I have tried to analyze the situation from a viewpoint of what is right or wrong, what is healthy or unhealthy, what is normal or abnormal, and whether I have a desire to change and why. At this point, I can manage my life, which consists of work, school and social activities. I feel I have control of my circumstances and have no reason to change. I accept the health risks of having multiple lovers and enjoy my life as it is.

"In trying to understand how I became this way. I look back to my family circumstances and my childhood. My father was an alcoholic and spent little time at home. I grew up in a medium-sized town where outward behavior was supposed to be prim and proper, but everyone had hidden lives doing whatever they could get away with.

"At about seven years of age, I became the youngest member of a group of teens and pre-teens who ran around together and did fun things. One of the fun things the older boys did was to introduce the girls to sex. I was introduced at eight years of age. By the time I was eleven, sex was a regular part of our gang activities, and I began to enjoy it. From then on, it seemed sex was the subject that occupied most of my thoughts. I feel lucky I didn't get pregnant or contract any sexually transmitted diseases. Maybe I can't get pregnant. I have never tried to, but I am beginning to think it would be nice to have a baby before I am 40.

"I think the tendency to become addicted to something is inherited, and the environment determines what we become addicted to. I feel addicted to sex, but I really don't have any good reason to want to break this addiction. Am I looking at this realistically? Is there another way of looking at this from a wellness perspective which I should consider?"

My response to her story was to suggest exploring her questions with a counselor, psychologist or sex therapist. As a wellness educator and coach, this was outside my expertise.

****

Storge: Love in the Mental Dimension— The Storge Climax

"Love is a decision," I've heard several speakers say. I think one component of love is rational decision making. Storge conveys the concept of conscious decisions to live up to obligations and promises. If you parent a child, you have an obligation to provide support, nurture, and safety regardless of how the child's behavior or appearance makes you feel. If you take vows and make promises, you are obligated to make decisions to protect the relationship, regardless of the temptations that arise.

Storge love is a step above eros love. Eros depends on biologic drives while storge is anchored in thinking and deciding.

Since eros has set the order of analysis of love, let's start with reproduction.

Reproduction

Just as eros love is the trigger for producing offspring, storge love is the trigger for creativity. Products of the mind are tangibles and intangibles left behind when you are no more. The storge climax—the surge of euphoria when something new is conceived in the mind and brought to fruition—may come before and/ or after the product becomes a reality. The brain chemistry is similar to what coordinates the erotic climax but not as dramatic in intensity, and more variable in duration.

Some creative people create and enjoy only for themselves, but products of creativity bring the most joy when they are shared. New music and lyrics, poetry, inventions, books, gadgets, knowledge, ideas, instruments, medicines, etc. are first conceived in the mind or stumbled upon in pursuit of solutions to life's challenges.

GROWTH

The stages of growth in decision making follow the physiologic growth cycle—from infancy to old age. Instinct and impulse are regulated as abilities for analysis and rational behavior develop. The process of gathering data, looking at options, projecting outcomes, and selecting an option with the best risk/benefit ratio is well established. Intuition and "gut instinct" in decisions are highly individualized. Wisdom is the accumulation of lessons from what works and what doesn't work in life decisions.

Storge love undergirds all these processes. We sometimes forget the love component of decision making.

REST

Decision making about relationships require work—see next subtopic. We can't engage the mind in structured tasks all the time. It needs breaks and reprieve from responsibilities. It needs diversion, relaxation, and sleep. Sleep is more important for the mind than for the body.

WORK

Storge's work means putting effort and energy into analyzing relationships, and purposefully making decisions to improve. This includes an effort to control the negative emotional component of dealing with relationships. It also includes the hard work of actively seeking to restore or repair broken relationships.

NUTRITION

The food for storge love includes successful decision making, finding solutions to problems, rational control of emotions, and learning from the examples and stories of others. The ability to search for credible, reliable information, and to discriminate between pseudoscience and good data, is food for storge. (In a later chapter, we will expand on this and explore the "mindfulness" strategies that can strengthen and enhance these qualities.)

HOMEOSTASIS—BALANCE

The balance storge helps to establish and maintain is between decision making and no decision making, between good and bad decisions, and between letting emotions or reason dominate. It is important to balance impulsive gut instincts with following the data. Successful applications of storge love calls for accepting our imperfections while striving for growth, fulfilling our obligations while practicing self-care, and grieving loss while celebrating gains.

Recovering from a broken heart—loss of romantic love—is a good example of where this balance is needed. Time alone doesn't heal. A rational reappraisal of the circumstances and the personalities involved has been shown to help. In his book *How to Fix a Broken Heart,* psychologist, Guy Winch recommends the mental technique called "negative reappraisal—an analytical process of reviewing the broken relationship in a balanced approach more consistent with reality."[7]

****

Philia: Love in the Psychosocial Dimension—The Philial Climax

The love of philia is a deeply felt affection for another person. This affection confers value, worth, need, caring, esteem, shared pleasure, and mutual support in pain. This is the love of a heart-felt, deep friendship, a love without eros. But when philia has the same object as eros, the partner/spouse is a best friend. This is a beautiful relationship. Friends carry each other in their heart, mind, and spirit.

Reproduction

The love of philia forms mirror images in each friend's mind, and the memories survive each other's demise. When the bonds of friendship survive the ups and downs of life, when mutual hurts are healed, and when periodic separation cannot dull esteem for one another, that is philial love. When you summarize the relationship as "I cannot imagine my life without you in it," that is the philial climax, the merging of two personalities into one complementary whole. "You complete me," is quite applicable.

Building strong bonds of friendship requires time, pleasant communication styles, shared likings, enjoyable activities, shared confidences, trust, mutual forgiveness, dependability and mutual esteem.[8, 9] So, the analogous experience is a quiet conclusion over time, not an explosive, short-lived event of bioelectricity, nor the sudden dawning of a creative moment. The philial climax is a summary conclusion over time that "this person has a special place in my life." The brain chemistry for this climatic pleasure is much more reserved and drawn out. I believe that similar brain chemicals are involved but at lower levels and possibly in differing combinations.

GROWTH

Philial love is rooted in the value of self subconsciously absorbed by the newborn's brain. Through the senses of touch, hearing, and later sight, a newborn's brain gets information about the safety and security of its environment. This establishes a set-point for self-esteem and confidence with which the child faces the world.[10]

Psychosocial growth accompanies physical growth. The teenage years and early adulthood are the most important stages of growth that adjust the set-point up or down to establish and maintain friendships. Beautiful stories are told of lifelong friendships that began in childhood. They all illustrate the truism: "a true friend loves at all times—not just when things are going well."[9]

REST

Philial love needs breaks, time apart for self-care, and reflection. However, true friends do find rest and relaxation even in each other's presence. Long periods of silence for individual solitude can be very comfortable even when you are side by side. Time spent together does not have to be filled with activity and conversation every moment.

WORK

Philial love requires effort, planning, thoughtfulness, and caring. It may need reminders before becoming automatic. No good thing gets created, or lasts, without effort. The work to build and maintain a friendship is part of the joy of the experience.

Stress Adaptation

Philial love provides emotional and material support as needed. This includes help to explore options and rescue when needed. This love is like a lightning rod to diffuse the thunderstorms in life.

Nutrition

What is food for philial love? There are three answers: communication, communication, communication. Whether in person, via social media, or old-fashioned letter writing, communication is the key to nurture philial love.

Homeostasis —Balance

The balance to be maintained is between self and the other. Healthy friendships call for maintenance of identity and finding a third identity in the relationship. Most friendships call for adjustments over time so one is not more dominant, nor always giving in to the other. Willingness to reach a compromise, take turns, forgive, discard hurts and slights, and grow together are all balancing acts that contribute to the richness of a deep friendship.

****

AGAPE: LOVE IN THE SPIRITUAL DIMENSION—THE AGAPE CLIMAX

The best definition we have of agape love is unconditional, selfless love hinting at perfect love. This is most times referred to as "God's love," or akin to the love of God.

To be fair to our treatment of love, we cannot shift to exploring God's love when we started with human love on the most basic level. So, we'll look at agape love as not fully seen in humans, but as an ideal to strive to attain.

REPRODUCTION

How does agape love evoke a climatic experience in humans that may lead to "reproducing offspring?" In our discussion groups, we were privileged to get input on this question from a wide range of belief systems.

Atheists said the wonder of the vastness and complexities of the universe brings a breath-taking pause as you acknowledge the insignificance of one human being. There are laws not yet discovered that may code for guidance, order, and design—a GOD.

Buddhists said when you reach Nirvana—the end of desire—there is only inner peace, joy, and freedom. Birth, age, sickness, pain, and death cease to exist.

Christians said God is love and seeks out humans to partake of that love by "practicing God's presence and walking in His love." Worship and prayer strengthen these bonds.

Hindus said the main goal of life is union with Brahman, ultimate reality. In Brahman, there is no sense of individuality, only pure being, consciousness, and bliss.

Muslims said Muhammad's purpose in life was to call humans to return to the worship of the God of Abraham. This restoration of true faith calls for total surrender, which results in inner peace.

Jews said obedience to God's laws and acceptance of His rulership is the ultimate in relationship with God, and worship creates the closest bonds.

From this brief review, it is evident that most humans have some concept of a relationship with a higher power that is more mysterious than anything known on Earth. In that relationship, there is an experience of oneness that comes through understanding and accepting the call to grow into full agape love. Christianity has been the major promoter of the concept of agape love. The "oneness" is experienced as a slow development, or a sudden, dramatic "conversion" experience.

This oneness with God leads to the challenge of sharing that belief and drawing others into experiencing the same. Practicing being in the presence of God is the agape climax—the ultimate in a spiritual love relationship. Getting other people to desire that relationship and share in the practice is spiritual reproduction. In this climatic experience, there is spiritual pleasure.

The brain chemistry of this experience is similar to the other forms of pleasure. However, agape pleasure is based on beliefs, confidence in those beliefs, and living with them as a main compass for life. For humans, this ideal love is a beacon for continuous growth.

GROWTH

> AGAPE LOVE POINTS US TO IDEALS TO WHICH WE ASPIRE.

Human love can never be without flaws, for our humanity is flawed. Agape love points to ideals to which we aspire. Love without jealousy that is pure in intent, kind, just, merciful, gentle, unselfish, and not hasty to condemn. This is the result of growth over a lifetime—becoming but never fully achieving.

REST

Spiritual rest means inner peace. Agape love provides spiritual refuge, encouragement, hope, and assurance.

WORK

What sort of work is required of agape love? This can be the effort to control negative impulses, bridle offensive language, seek forgiveness, forgive, stand up for the downtrodden, feed the hungry, and be kind especially to those in need. This work is energized by more than knowledge and decision making. It is done empowered by beliefs in altruism and service to humanity.

STRESS ADAPTATION

Agape love calms the soul, cleanses life's mistakes through forgiveness, and restores worth and value when lost. Rituals in various religions, and some non-religious practices reduce misunderstandings, restore relationships, and heal the spirit.

NUTRITION

The food for agape love is worship, contemplation of the cosmos, and meditation on things of eternal value. Worship, prayer, and music feed the spirit.

HOMEOSTASIS—BALANCE

Agape love regards all humans as equal and worthwhile. The balance between self and others is lifted to a higher level with the perspective of transcendental worth. Balance also calls for avoiding fanaticism and exclusivity.

****

Now that we completed our survey of the four loves, let's share some applications to our lives. Do you remember the first time you felt "in love?" The first girlfriend? The first boyfriend?

Well, here's my memory:

I was 11 and in love for the first time. The girl was in a lower grade, so we never had a chance to sit together in class. However, during the two weeks for final exams, all the grades mixed in alternate seating to reduce cheating in a one-room school. The seats were long wooden benches, so if you are helping a student sitting by you as you prepare for an exam, you can really lean in and experience closeness. You can hide her pencil, or otherwise tease.

A few months before this major stroke of luck came my way, I had broken my leg and spent three months in the hospital. The bone healed, but the site, mid-thigh, was sensitive to pressure. After any teasing or hiding her paper or pencil, I was rewarded with closed fists pounding on my healed leg bone. Ah, delicious pain, sweet fists! Pleasant memories of childhood love!

****

Pleasure and Pain

A brief overview of pleasure and pain may also give us greater perspectives on love, wellness, and happiness.

How do you define pleasure or pain? We know when we have it, but it's hard to put into words.

Pleasure is the perception of pleasant and enjoyable stimuli. This may vary in degree from the state of existing without pain—the baseline—to euphoric states of climactic ecstasy. That euphoric state may overwhelm the consciousness and cause fainting.

In human experience, pleasure may be immediate, short-term, long-term, or delayed. We can use the word "gratification" as a synonym for pleasure, but it carries an additional meaning of self-centered pleasure. And we can examine pleasure, as a mode of human experience, without evaluation based on beliefs and religious teachings. However, we must consider the final integration of pleasure as a personal experience within the context of individual beliefs and values.

Immediate pleasures produce pleasant feelings described by such terms as thrilling, surge of joy, climactic, euphoric, or ecstatic, occurring over a short time frame—from an instant to a few hours. "Immediate" refers to the short time between the stimulus and the response. A taste of honey and other sensory pleasures are immediate.

Short-term pleasures produce the same feelings over a few days to weeks. The mechanism is the same, but the intensity of the response may not be as high as immediate. The enjoyment of a short vacation when everything goes well is an example.

Long-term pleasures are those derived from planning and working toward a reward over months and years. Most times, we achieve the reward through postponement of immediate and short-term pleasures. Sometimes, the unexpected positive results from working at otherwise unexciting tasks produce the most pleasure in the long run. This happens in doing work necessary to achieve certain goals, while putting aside activities that might be pleasurable but not directly contributing to the goal.[6] Setting a goal to write a book and seeing it come to fruition is an example.

Pain is the perception of unpleasant, hurtful feelings sometimes called "noxious stimuli." The word "noxious," means harmful or hurtful. Though we mostly use this to reference physical pain, the same meaning is useful for pain in the other dimensions.

Common words to describe pain are acute, chronic, or referred. Acute pain is immediate or short term, while chronic pain remains longer—days, weeks, years. Referred pain means the sensation of pain is felt in one location in the body, but the cause of the pain is elsewhere.

In terms of quality, words to describe pain include sharp, dull, throbbing, crushing, and excruciating. Pain may be so severe it can overwhelm the consciousness and produce fainting.

Pain in the physiologic dimension is always a signal of something abnormal. It serves as a warning of potential or actual tissue damage, abnormal pressure or spasm in organs, or actual death of tissue. This pain is the easiest to understand because it is a protective mechanism for the physical body. Unless you have hereditary insensitivity to pain or damaged nerves, you have felt physiologic pain and understand its function.

Mental pain originates in the mind's ability to handle information. This "hurting" may derive from the perception and interpretation of information received from others. It may be triggered by personal memories of past hurts, guilt, regrets, or self-blame. The knowledge and awareness of mistakes, missed opportunities, wrong decisions, loss, and misuse or lack of information can produce mental pain that feels just as real as physical pain. The sensation or quality of the pain is different because it does not originate in tissue damage. It originates in the mind's capacity to process and interpret information.

Psychosocial pain has to do with the negative valuation of self and self-perception. Thus, shyness and self-consciousness, low self-esteem, lack of confidence, devaluing treatment from others, feelings of embarrassment, shame, and disgrace may produce pain as real and with similar effects as if tissue or organ damage occurred.

The quality of the pain is different from physical pain but the effects on the person are just as real. As we shall see later, these psychological effects have real biological consequences.

Spiritual pain has to do with the lack of purpose and meaning, feelings of hopelessness and despair, and the transcendent questions of life. The origin of this pain is in the mind's capacity to define and seek meaning, purpose, and satisfaction in life.

Pleasure and pain, and the motivational drives in all aspects of life, could be a take-off for your book. Cathy Gere's *Pleasure, Pain and the Greater Good* may stir your creativity in that direction.[6]

****

STORY: PLEASURE, PAIN, AND FORGIVENESS—MY SECOND GIRLFRIEND.

She was 14, and I was 16. It was normal teenage love while it lasted. The breakup was the sad, painful, regrettable part. I had a naturally hot, nasty temper. In a gossipy culture, someone said something and told someone else who then spread it around within our circle of teenage friends. It triggered my impulsive, angry reaction, and I hit her—in the presence of a group of mutual friends!

The very moment after the incident, regret and remorse washed over me. I had committed the most grievous sin of my whole life, but I was too proud to ask for forgiveness. Five years later, I left the community without having asked for forgiveness, or apologizing for my assault.

Fifty-five years later, I received a phone call from her.

"I called to say I have forgiven you." Oh, what a huge relief. We talked about *the incident* and how it had affected her feelings about herself from that time on into her adult life. I voiced my apologies and how I wished it had never happened. I acknowledged my hot temper and how the incident made me resolve never to hit another woman.

She continued, "It took a lot of courage on my part not knowing what the outcome of my phone call might be. I feel happier now for taking the initiative to reconnect and let you know I had forgiven you."

Ah, I wish many others can have these kinds of experiences—forgiveness ceremonies. We all hurt one another. Victim or perpetrator, offering, asking, and accepting forgiveness is love, wellness, and happiness in action.

We have been good friends since then—comfortable friends, comparing notes on children, grandchildren, and aging.

****

STORY: THE SCAR THAT WILL NEVER GO AWAY: MY HOT TEMPER AND THE JOY OF ASKING FORGIVENESS

I was maybe 12 years old. One Saturday afternoon, my brother who was four years older, a mutual friend, and I were sitting on the bed in the guest room of our home. As older brothers like to do, he was teasing me about a girlfriend. Our friend was laughing, and I was getting angrier by the second. On an impulse, I grabbed a double-edged razor blade left on the windowsill and slashed him across the left thigh!

It was a deep cut, about seven inches long, just at the point where his shorts ended. He grabbed the edges of the wound to stop the bleeding. Our eldest brother rushed him off to the clinic where he got it stitched up—without any local anesthesia.

Over the years, we have joked about it, tried to understand our sibling conflicts, and told our children and grandchildren about our wild behavior. But I had never told him I was sorry.

Sixty-two years after the incident, I felt I needed to say "I'm sorry." I called him up and opened the conversation.

"About that scar on your left leg . . ."

"Yes, I see it every day since I only wear shorts in this tropical weather."

"I never said I'm sorry. Today, I've called to say I'm sorry, and to ask your forgiveness for the result of that flash of hot-temper."

We talked for an hour and reviewed other mishaps and misunderstandings growing up as seven brothers who fought each other on many occasions. We ended with, "It feels good to say I'm sorry, and it's good to hear you say you forgive me."

I'll see the scar again next time we visit, but this time it will have a different meaning to us.

****

STORY: A RELIGIOUS RITUAL THAT RESTORED A RELATIONSHIP

In the introduction to this book, I recalled getting angry with the business manager at the college where I had my first teaching job. Well, several years later, we attended the same church. It seemed that we avoided each other for many years—it was a large congregation.

One of the special services at church included a segment called "The Ordinance of Humility." The congregation separated into different rooms according to gender and age. We then partnered and washed each other's feet. The group sang familiar hymns, and each set of partners prayed for each other.

When I entered the room for men on one such occasion, my former colleague and I came face-to-face. As our eyes met, the same question escaped our lips almost simultaneously: "Shall we?"

We did. As we took turns washing each other's feet, we got caught up with our stories since our last conversation. He had retired. I had gotten a job with the heart surgeons at Washington Hospital Center at a salary three times what I made at the college. We expressed mutual regret for how the business transaction happened and reflected on the lessons we had learned from it. We agreed that this ritual had practical benefits for love, wellness, and happiness. We parted as friends.

****

C. S. Lewis's book was published in 1960. Since then, humanistic and positive psychology have researched many aspects of love and added some new terminology to the discourse. Terms such as companionate love, romantic love, compassionate love, and adult attachment love are being studied and explained. Research on these topics has inspired numerous articles and books. Pain-free love is the goal even while acknowledging that there is no love without pain, and the pain of loving enriches love.[11, 12]

Peruse the items in the Notes (Appendix 5), when you have time. Maybe you will write the next best-seller on love!

NOTES FOR YOUR BOOK

_____

_____

_____

_____

_____

_____

_____

_____

_____

_____

_____

_____

_____

_____

_____

_____

_____

_____

_____

_____

_____

3

HEALTHCARE—
FROM PSEUDOSCIENCE
TO WELLNESS

To love or have loved, that is enough.
Ask nothing further. There is no other pearl
to be found in the dark folds of life.

—Victor Hugo

This chapter will briefly review how our knowledge about the world around us changed between the end of the eighteenth century and current day. As our knowledge increased, our understanding of how the body works also increased. We changed our practices of taking care of people in sickness and in health.

The diagram below captures the major concepts on which eighteenth-century medicine operated.[1] Look at the circle and note the arrows that point to the north, south, east, and west. The highlights in this diagram are the beliefs that

1. The four elements—air, earth, fire, and water—could describe all matter. Air is the opposite of earth, and fire is the opposite of water. (Remember, this was long before the periodic table of elements.)
2. Among the four elements, there were four qualities with each pair being opposites: hot and cold, wet and dry.
3. There were four humors (fluids) in the body—blood, yellow bile, black bile, and phlegm.
4. The four organs regulating these fluids were: heart—blood, liver—yellow bile, spleen—black bile, and brain—phlegm.
5. Depending on which fluid was dominant, behavior could be classified as sanguine (blood), choleric (yellow bile), melancholic (black bile), and phlegmatic (phlegm).
6. To treat disease, a physician would try to regulate the body fluids, use the hot-cold, wet-dry processes to combat symptoms, and bleed the patient to get rid of excess fluids.

As we look back at eighteenth-century medicine, it is easy to see that before the scientific method was established, beliefs and practices were what prominent "thinkers" felt, reasoned, or deduced from the prevailing conditions. We should call this "The Unscientific Model" of healthcare. Bloodletting, use of leeches, and belief in "miasmas" gave way as chemists began to understand the structure of matter. John Dalton gave his explanations of atoms and how they combine to make up other compounds between 1803 and 1810.[2]

The work of Koch, Lister, and Pasteur in the 1830s to 1870s set the stage for a rational approach to understanding nature.[2] By 1910, the scientific method for establishing facts through experimentation was widely accepted.

The classification of temperaments as sanguine, choleric, melancholic, and phlegmatic still persists. A quick Google search of these terms reveals a host of books and seminars that are still peddled as helpful. They do not use the body fluid foundation, but they still use the same behavioral qualities to categorize people. It seems to me if the foundation is in pseudoscience, we should discard the product when science has other explanations and terminology.

Here's a summary of what the science of the eighteenth century believed about nature and human function.

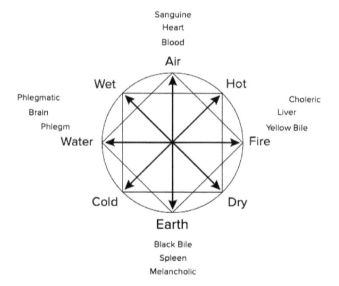

The Eighteenth Century Unified Model of Healthcare

The unified model of matter, health states and body function which influenced the practice of medicine in the eighteenth century. This model was the basis for the first personality type indicator
(Adapted from Ackerkneckt, 1982)

THE SCIENTIFIC MODELS OF HEALTHCARE

In 1910, the Carnegie Foundation for the Advancement of Teaching issued what has become known as the Flexner Report on medical education in the United States and Canada.[3] The main point of this report was that medical schools should teach and use only facts and methods supportable by the scientific method. The scientific method called for testing a possible explanation, being objective about the test results, and repeating tests by others to see the results were reproducible.

THE BIOMEDICAL MODEL

The standards set in the Flexner Report changed medical education from "a barbershop type of operation where anybody with the money could get it," to a training in the disciplines of science. There were qualifications required to enter medical schools. Knowledge was based on verifiable information gained through experimentation.[3]

Healthcare became a process of treating disease with drugs and surgery. This model prioritized the disease processes and the diseased organs over the patient as a human being.

THE PSYCHOSOMATIC MODEL

In the 1930s, a group of psychiatrists began to promote the idea that the mind and body interact in all disease processes. They called attention to the fact that a patient's psychological stress, genetics, behaviors, and environment should be considered in treating any illness.[4]

However, the 1940s through the 1960s was a time of major biomedical innovation with the discovery of the structure of DNA. This brought more prominence to the scientific model, and the psychosomatic model lost some steam.

THE BIOPSYCHOSOCIAL MODEL

In 1977, George Engel proposed a new model to include the psychology and environment of the patient. Since this was an addition to the biomedical model, he called it the biopsychosocial model.[5] Other researchers added ethnic and cultural factors. This model became the foundation for the specialty of Family Medicine.

THE HOLISTIC MODEL

This model became popular in the late 1970s as "alternative medicine" was on the rise. The key idea here was health and healing should treat the object of care as a whole individual with a culture, needs, a set of beliefs and practices, and a set of relationships. Care for the whole person should include prevention, diagnosis, treatment, rehab, and optimizing function. The American Holistic Medical Association, founded in 1978, seems to be defunct and has been succeeded by the Foundation for Alternative and Integrative Medicine.[6]

The rise in popularity of alternative medicine became a consumer phenomenon. People were willing to try other treatments besides drugs and surgery. By 1990 consumers were spending around $13 billion annually out-of-pocket to try alternative treatments.[7] By 2012, that figure was $30 billion.

THE HEALTH PROMOTION MODEL

As the healthcare industry and medical schools struggled to catch up with consumer demands, The Office of Disease Prevention and Health Promotion was established within the US Public Health Service. The emphasis on "Healthy People" became the focus of national initiatives to prevent disease and promote health.

The first "Healthy People" report was issued in 1979. Since then, there has been a plan for each subsequent decade of effort and data collection. Beginning with Healthy People 1990, followed by Healthy People 2000, national objectives, plans to reach the objectives, and data tracking are run each decade to improve prevention and health promotion strategies. This is done with public input channeled through the Office of Disease Prevention and Health Promotion.[8]

THE WELLNESS MODEL

Again, the public has been ahead of institutions and government in adopting terminology that connects with their needs. "Wellness" was a word used on the fringes of healthcare to mean optimum health, function, and satisfaction with life. It has now become part of the mainstream in health education, traditional healthcare, medical schools, and in alternative medicine. Just about every institution now has a Wellness Department, Wellness Office, Wellness Clinic, or something else with "Wellness" in its name.[9]

****

It was not too long ago (around 2005) when I sat on a committee to change the name of a department at a university from "Department of Health Sciences and Physical Education" to "Department of Health, Wellness, and Physical Education."

> WELLNESS IS THE PRODUCT OF THE EFFORT AND ATTITUDES WE BRING TO THE PROCESS OF LIVING THE BEST LIFE POSSIBLE.

The definition of wellness that captures all the angles for me is: "Wellness is the product of the effort and attitudes we bring to the process of living the best life possible."

When living the best life possible, we need the best disease prevention methods, healing modalities, rehab services, optimization of our abilities, and fulfillment in life. Our attitude and effort decide where we put ourselves on the scale from low to high level wellness.

The diagram on the next page puts all these models into perspective with a timeframe and the organizations that champion their views. It is important to note that the best of the past has been brought forward to build the best for the present. The Biomedical Model was established by the birth of the scientific method. The Psychosomatic Model gave us mind/body integration. The Biopsychosocial Model gave us behavioral medicine. The Holistic Model gave us whole person healthcare. The Health Promotion Model emphasized prevention. The Wellness Model is promoting all of that on a foundation of love with the outcome of happiness.

It took 100 years to go from acceptance of a scientific approach to healthcare to get to a complete model—The Wellness Model.

Evolution of the Healthcare Model

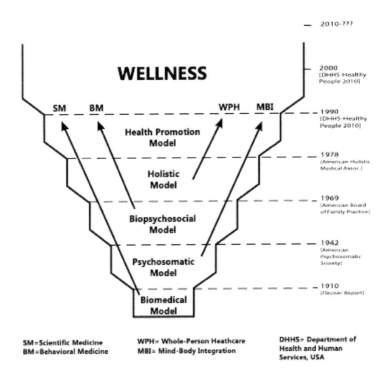

This next illustration shows as we go through life from birth to death, we are in one of three different states of health: the absence of disease, having signs and symptoms, or having a definite disease. As we go through each health state, we can have the attitudes and put in the effort to have high-level or low-level wellness. That summarizes the Wellness Model of healthcare across the life span. It is difficult to see how to improve this model.

Wellness and Health States Over Time

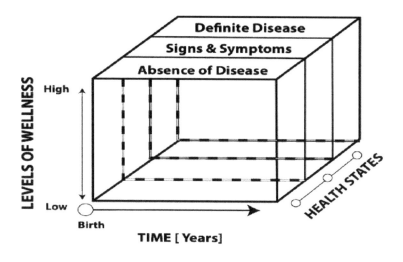

****

My first major encounter with the healthcare system was as an inpatient for three months in the hospital in Kingstown, St. Vincent. I was ten years old. The incident stuck in my memory is about a new Matron of Nursing (equivalent to today's Director of Nursing) trying to regulate patients' bowel and bladder functions. In my earlier telling of this story (in *Personal Wellness: How to Go the Distance*), I titled it "To Pee or Not to Pee."

One of the policies our new Matron instituted was to pass bedpans and urinals to the bedridden patients only at set times of the day. The schedule was three times a day, right after meals. If one of us needed the use of these implements at other times, we had to hold it for the next scheduled time of service.

We were on an open ward of about 40 beds. The bed next to mine was occupied by a gentleman around 55 years of age. Mr. King had broken one leg while working at the docks in Kingstown.

One day, he needed to use a urinal and was told he had to wait for about two hours according to the schedule. He told the nurses he couldn't wait and if they didn't want a wet floor, they would bring him a urinal right then. The nurses felt they had to stick to the rules and denied him the "pee-jug," as it was known on the ward. With one leg in the traction apparatus, Mr. King pulled himself off the side of the bed, unwrapped his pajama bottoms, and proceeded to wet the floor.

Of course, this triggered a rapid response from the nurses. One ran to get a pee-jug, and another hurriedly brought a screen to put around Mr. King's bed. One ran to get a mop, and a fourth kept a lookout for the Matron.

******

The other incident from that hospitalization that stuck with me was the embarrassment of a ten-year-old to be in traction without pajama bottoms. The day my teacher brought the whole class to visit me was especially challenging to keep my genitals covered with only a pajama top. And my first girlfriend was in the group that came to visit!

******

The Wellness Model will not try to regulate a patient's bowel and bladder needs. It would be sensitive to the need for proper coverage in an open ward, even for a pre-pubescent boy.

Another incident in our lives highlighting the need for healthcare reform was the struggle to pay huge hospital bills when we didn't have health insurance in the 1980s. I was unemployed. My wife needed back surgery due to a fall. By the time the bills were due, we had no income, and no health insurance.

The hospital's business manager took an interest in our case, and got our bills paid under a federal provision called "The

Hill-Burton Act." I didn't know who Hill and Burton were, but they saved us from major financial disaster.

****

As you contemplate this brief overview of how healthcare has changed over the course of 110 years, what experiences and stories come to mind?

NOTES FOR YOUR BOOK

_____

_____

_____

_____

_____

_____

_____

_____

_____

_____

_____

_____

_____

_____

_____

4

THE PERSONAL PURSUIT OF HAPPINESS

Love is the greatest refreshment in life.

—Pablo Picasso

My beliefs include these general statements:

o   All humans want to love and be loved.
o   All humans want to be happy.

I believe these are universal truths—we are hard-wired that way.

The French included a statement on happiness in their 1789 document "Declaration of the Rights of Man and of the Citizen."[1] It contains this statement: "The goal of society is common happiness."

Thomas Jefferson is credited for the inclusion of "the pursuit of happiness" as one of the inalienable rights mentioned in the US Declaration of Independence. The debate about *inalienable* versus *unalienable* isn't important here.[2] More important is our misperception if we think *pursuit* meant *chase*. The usage of *pursuit* referred more to *practicing* or *experiencing* happiness.[3] Jefferson had input on the French document, which became one of the foundational pieces sparking the French Revolution.

Are you happy? Are you in pursuit of—practicing, exercising—happiness? Let's check:

Answer the five questions below as honestly as you can, with no long contemplation over particular events or people.

Here are five statements you may agree or disagree with. Using the 1–7 scale below, indicate your agreement with each item by placing the appropriate number on the line preceding that item. Please be open and honest in your responses.

- o   7—Strongly agree
- o   6—Agree
- o   5—Slightly agree
- o   4—Neither agree nor disagree
- o   3—Slightly disagree
- o   2—Disagree
- o   1—Strongly disagree

— In most ways my life is close to my ideal.
— The conditions of my life are excellent.
— I am satisfied with my life.
— So far, I have gotten the important things I want in life.
— If I could live my life over, I would change almost nothing.

(*Used with permission from the creators.*)[4]

Your score: Add up all the numbers you placed in front of the five statements. Compare the total with this distribution:

Your score =

o   31–35 Extremely satisfied
o   26–30 Satisfied
o   21–25 Slightly satisfied
o   20   Neutral
o   15–19 Slightly dissatisfied
o   10–14 Dissatisfied
o   5–9 Extremely dissatisfied

The above questionnaire is called the "The Satisfaction with Life Scale (SWLS). It has over 30 years of validation and use in research all over the world. It's primary author, Dr. Ed Diener, is currently on the faculty at the University of Virginia and the University of Utah, and is known worldwide as "Dr. Happiness."[5]

****

For the segment on happiness in my health and wellness courses, I would draw from scholarly writings and the current "positive psychology" research. Here are a few thoughts from some of the experts in the late 1990s as used in my courses.

Again, let me voice my disclaimer. I am not an expert or scholar of the social sciences, and I see my role as a layperson, facilitator of thinking and self-examination. I have come to a particular place in history at a particular time when there is academic freedom and encouragement to be innovative. To this task, I bring a particular synthesis of ideas and experiences; I love teaching but dislike doing empirical research.

My goal is to stimulate personal introspection to promote personal wellness. In doing so, I must be aware of the discussions and ideas of experts and share in a synthesis compatible with a model that addresses the needs of the whole person.

The following sources have reinforced the need to address this subject. They also provide perspectives and ideas with which to fulfill the task. I recommend a careful reading of these three books. They give a broad survey of the philosophical roots of our definition of happiness, summarize the then current research on happy people, and the reasons they are happy. Their research data have been supported by later studies in the field of positive psychology.

In Pursuit of Happiness, published by the University of Notre Dame Press in 1995, is a collection of lectures in the series "Boston University Studies in Philosophy and Religion." This is a joint project between the Boston University Institute for Philosophy and Religion, and the University of Notre Dame Press.[6]

In their thought-provoking styles, philosophers like Charles Griswold of Boston University, Margaret Miles of Harvard Divinity School, Huston Smith of Syracuse University, and Tu Wei-Ming of Harvard University present their definitions of happiness and the ramifications for personal living. This volume must be digested slowly. It is pleasure reading of a high order—solid mental nutrition.

Here are some definitions and summaries from the discussion:

1. Long-term happiness is tranquility—not emptiness but a dynamic rest, which has overcome deep anxieties about life's greatest questions.
2. Happiness is desire and delight in the interconnectedness of all things in an immensely generous universe.
3. Happiness is not only pleasure, but a blessedness where paradoxical states like happiness and unhappiness are blended in a "peace that passes all understanding." The positive absorbs the negative state.

4. Joy is not quite happiness, for "joy is a sensation which surges through us when we are doing especially well at what we are good at doing."

5. Happiness is joyful performance of God's will, integrating spiritual joy and enlightenment with selfless altruistic concern for the happiness of others.

6. Happiness is satisfaction derived from gaining one's humanity where harmony with nature and with heaven leads to participatory joy in building up the community.

7. Leroy S. Rouner, the editor of this volume, writes a closing to the introduction to which summarizing would not do justice, so here, I quote two paragraphs and hope this qualifies for fair use and more publicity for this volume, which has been a delight to read.

> All of which reminds us that the point of reflecting on happiness is to learn how to be happy, and perhaps to remind us that we are luckier than we realize. At the least, we all have brief moments of joy. And we all have the reflective opportunity, which Charles Griswold celebrates, for a rationally ordered life in which we take responsibility for our choices, and have the satisfaction of trust that we have chosen well. Those of us who are religious have had moments of God-given ecstasy; and, most of all, we know something of Huston Smith's deep assurance that nothing in Heaven or Earth can finally separate us from the love of God, and that we are therefore truly among the blessed.

> And even for those who are not religious, but who are sensitive to the life of the world around them, there is what Margaret Miles has called the Great Beauty, the realization that the world in its benign

generosity can be lovely beyond any singing of it. In these times of tragedy and trouble, that alone is enough to give us an Augustinian "glimpse" of what it means to be truly happy.

****

Happiness and the Limits of Satisfaction, written by Deal W. Hudson, is a concise review of the philosophical evolution of the meaning of "happiness."[7] Dr. Hudson was an associate professor of philosophy at Fordham University. He takes a strong stance against the popular, common definition of happiness in terms of feelings alone. He reviews the traditional meanings which seem to have been lost from the definition, and from modern life.

Dr. Hudson calls the popular definition of happiness "well-feeling, a subjective, self-reported psychological state, subject to misinterpretation and self-deception." He passionately argues for the re-inclusion of "eudaimonia," from the Greek word for happiness, which carries the meaning of "moral virtue in a life capable of objective signs of happiness—objective in terms of being observable and desirable by others."

"Happiness," he writes, "belongs to those who, given their humanity and their circumstances, have distinguished themselves to their friends by their steadfast and successful commitment to the life they envision."

A few chapter titles may entice you to read this book. Again, this book provides high nutritive value for the mind, and is better enjoyed slowly. In chapters such as "Popular Views of Happiness," "The Rejection of Psychological Happiness," "The Enigma of Jefferson's Pursuit," "Happiness and Pain" and "The Passion for Happiness," Hudson reasons the reader into an evaluation of definitions and personal applications of happiness.

Well-being, or "the state of our lives taken as a whole," is distinguished from *well-feeling,* which is "momentary and passing states of feeling."

A minimum moral code of behavior must be included in a happy life, or that is necessary to produce the happy life. Responsibilities may not create immediate feelings of psychological happiness, but they are part of a happy life.

Hudson presents a much-appreciated review of philosophy from Aristotle, Locke, Aquinas, and others. His quote from Aristotle is telling of his viewpoint.

> "HAPPINESS IS THE FINAL END FOR THE SAKE OF WHICH EVERYTHING ELSE IS DONE."—ARISTOTLE

"Happiness is the final end for the sake of which everything else is done."

He takes to task the preachers of positive thinking and visualization of "the good life" for recommending the "immediacy of feelings" over moral virtue, which produces longer-lasting feelings.

Here are a few of the major points of Dr. Hudson's treatise:

1. Ambiguity about the definition of happiness is caused by ambiguity about human nature.
2. The human desire for happiness cannot be avoided—it is "an intractable fact of human nature."
3. Happiness involves internal consistency, maintenance of a stable character, a reason to live, and a vision of the best possible life.
4. Subjective talk and appraisal of happiness may be escapist, self-deceiving, and complicated by mood, tactics of avoidance and denial, and "the angle of self-scrutiny."
5. Happiness consists of more than feelings. The legacy of the moral philosophers argues for inclusion of:
    o eudaimonia—moral virtue

> o euthumia—joy, gladness, cheerfulness and good-heartedness
> o ataraxia—freedom from disturbance or pain
> o beatitudo and felicitas—tranquility and peace, deep-down feelings of delight and satisfaction.

The happy moment must be distinguished from the happy life. Earthly happiness must be distinguished from transcendental happiness.

6. Pain is a teacher in the school of happiness, providing the opportunity for growth. But the wise do not seek out pain. When it comes, they recognize pain as an opportunity for self-mastery.

7. Jefferson's philosophy was based on the Christian ideal of God's will for humans to be happy. God made humans with the nature to desire happiness. But this happiness is also a call to moral virtue, leisure, freedom, and lack of ill-will toward others.

****

The Pursuit of Happiness: Who Is Happy—and Why is written by David G. Myers, PhD, a social psychologist at Hope College in Michigan.[8] He presents much of the research about well-being, life satisfaction, and quality of life. Here are 20 items summarized from this discussion. See whether your experience or knowledge agrees with these conclusions based on happiness research.

1. Well-being is subjective, but it is more than "well-feeling." It is sometimes called "subjective well-being" to emphasize this point—a pervasive sense that life is good.

2. More people report being happier than previously estimated. Earlier estimates were that 20% of Americans were happy. Actual reports show more like 80% are happy.

3. College students in the 1980s and 1990s rated financial success as more important than developing a meaningful life philosophy.
4. Above a certain basic need, higher income has little or no effect on increased happiness.
5. Attitude about income and possessions is more important than the absolute amount.
6. The proportion of reported happiness did not increase as personal wealth increased nationally in the USA between 1930 and 1991.
7. What we say influences what we think and feel; positive talk promotes positive attitudes.
8. Happiness is experienced at a deeper level of living between the highs and the lows in life.
9. We can make conscious efforts to build our core level of happiness by managing our expectations and comparisons. Traditions and rituals that encourage self-denial and sacrifice seem to contribute to this.
10. From teens to those over 65 years of age, the same percentage of the population (80%) in 16 nations report feeling satisfied with life.
11. The popular notions of unhappiness due to post-menopausal and "empty-nest syndrome" factors in women—and the instability of men in "mid-life crisis"—are not supported by large-scale research. Older people report just as much happiness and satisfaction with life as younger people.
12. The happiest senior citizens are actively religious, enjoy close relationships, have good health, sufficient income, and motivation to enjoy a variety of activities.
13. Whether you are a housewife, corporate CEO, construction worker, or file clerk, career happiness comes from work which is compatible with your interests and abilities, and which provides a sense of competence and accomplishment.

14. Women are twice as likely as men to suffer bouts of depression and to feel worried or frightened. Women report more intense joy and sadness and attempt suicide more often than men. However, men are two to three times more likely to succeed. Men are five times more likely to become alcoholic and eight times more likely to commit violent crimes than women.

15. Minority groups (ethnic, people with disabilities, women) in America have similar levels of self-esteem as do white males.

16. High self-esteem, a sense of personal control, optimism, and extroversion are the inner traits that correspond to positive mental attitudes and greater well-being.

17. Setting goals, immersing in an activity, paying attention to what is happening, and savoring immediate experiences make work and life more enjoyable.

18. A social support system consisting of close relationships, comfortable companionship, and an inner circle of loyal intimacy promote wellbeing and happiness.

19. The ingredients of a happy marriage are sex (quality over quantity), intimacy, equity, and growth.

20. A belief system that engenders something larger and outside of self contributes to coping, well-being, and happiness. Empirical science cannot study it all, nor can it be proved or disproved.

****

The summaries above should serve to whet the appetite for more of this kind of reading. There is not much more to say about happiness beyond what we have already explored. However, a restatement may be useful to connect our wellness framework to these principles.

On the physiologic level, we must learn to optimize health, prevent diseases, promote function, engage in leisure activities, obtain treatments, and undergo rehabilitation. All help to maintain the capacities to function without pain and restriction for as long as possible, and all contribute to overall happiness.

At the mental level, we develop our capacity to learn. We make decisions and choices, accept codes of conduct and virtue, develop self-discipline, and practice self-management. We set goals and envision positive outcomes. We work, play, create, and think. This gets work done, brings mental pleasures, and also contributes to happiness.

On the psychosocial level, we take our sense of self-value, evaluate it, and seek to increase it. We grow. We relate in interdependent circles, deal with other people and value them in a way that is consistent with our beliefs. We become part of other people's lives, participate in shared pleasure, and help soothe one another's pain. We contribute to the happiness of others, thereby enriching our own.

At the spiritual level, we define our purpose in life, choose our meaning, and believe or not believe in forces more powerful than anything we have known or experienced. We transcend ourselves and hope to transcend everything earthly and find answers to life's deepest questions. We find happiness—shared happiness for self and the community of humans.

On the whole, humans tend to be so optimistic about happiness that we still find it in the face of hardships, discouragement, loss, wars, crimes, violence, hurt, and neglect.

I believe our capacity for happiness is related to our capacity for love. Usually, we can't dictate falling in love. It happens. The early programming of the brain, pheromones, and mental, psychosocial, and spiritual codes and beliefs set us up for falling in love.

IF HAPPINESS IS SEEN AS A STATE TO STRIVE FOR AND GRASP, IT MAY REMAIN OUT OF REACH.

Maybe, this is something like falling into happiness. The philosophers I read agree that if happiness is seen as a state to strive for and grasp, it may remain out of reach. Happiness is better viewed as a byproduct of effort in life, which matches abilities, and grace that fits the personal belief system.

Some other thoughts, doubtless stimulated by the reading I have been doing over the past weeks, seem to beg to be included:

1. Happiness involves fighting to grow in goodness and to extinguish badness. To come to the end of life, whenever that might be, and believe "I have fought a good fight" is a happy summary. But it has to be an authentic fight—not a feigned battle.

2. Experimentation with life has a curious combination of excitement and deeply grounded happiness. Any experiment has risks of failure. Nevertheless, a personal "experiment with truth," as Gandhi said, is worth the risk of failure. Then, whatever the outcome, it is acceptable.

3. Balance between the ends and the means, the destination and the journey, personal virtue and public responsibility, individualism and the community are necessary for happiness.

4. It seems a lot of current lifestyles, in the words of Deal Hudson, "are wrapped up in self-consuming decadence and disdain for public responsibility. Happiness is surrendered for the trappings." These thoughts remind me of a story.

THE DOG AND HIS SHADOW

A smart dog would go to a butcher shop every day to receive a bone from the butcher. He had to cross a bridge to get home with his bone and had made the trip many times without mishap.

One day, he stopped on the bridge to look over into the water below and saw his reflection holding a bone that looked larger than the one he had.

All of a sudden, he dropped his bone, and plunged into the water to snatch the larger bone from his shadow. The real bone washed downstream out of reach. This smart dog spent many days searching for the shadow he saw in the water and forgot about the butcher shop.

The "trivialization of happiness," as Hudson puts it, "is only a shadow of the real thing."

****

Currently, there's a plethora of research on happiness and positive psychology. Here are a few names of more senior researchers in the field of positive psychology. The research topics include happiness, optimizing human potential, career fulfillment and productivity, character strengths and virtues, love, stress resistance, learned optimism, learned helplessness, loneliness, mindfulness, creativity, motivation, hope, forgiveness, courage, etc.

- o Ed Diener, PhD ("Dr. Happiness," widely known for simple research tools on happiness), The University of Virginia, University of Utah, University of Illinois (https://www.pursuit-of-happiness.org/history-of-happiness/ed-diener/)
- o Martin Seligman, PhD ("Father of Positive Psychology"), Positive Psychology Center, University of Pennsylvania (https://www.authentichappiness.sas.upenn.edu/faculty-profile/profile-dr-martin-seligman.)

o Richard S. Schwartz, MD & Jacqueline Olds, MD (husband & wife), Harvard Medical School (http://www. beacon.org/cw_contributorinfo.aspx?ContribID=594& Name=Richard+S.+Schwartz%2C+MD)

o Mihaly Csikszentmihalyi, PhD, Claremont Graduate University, CA (https://www.cgu.edu/people/mihaly-csikszentmihalyi/) (Known for establishing, researching, and publicizing the concept of "Flow.")

o Barbara Frederickson, PhD, University of North Carolina, Chapel Hill (https://www.pursuit-of-happiness.org/ history-of-happiness/barb-fredrickson/)

o Aaron T. Beck, MD, (https://beckinstitute.org/about-beck/ team/our-history/)

o Albert Bandura, PhD (94 years old!), (https://albertbandura. com/)

I could fill several pages with the researchers and practitioners of positive psychology. My aim here is to highlight a few of the leaders, particularly 94-year-old Dr. Albert Bandura. He gave us the concept of self-efficacy—the self-perception of how well we can function in a given situation.

I used some of their papers and books for concepts and exercises that fit into my wellness courses.

The younger generation of positive psychologists are spreading their knowledge and applications to the public via college courses, and free online classes.

In 2018, Dr. Laurie Santos launched an undergrad course "Psychology and the Good Life" (PSYC 157) at Yale University. It quickly became the most popular course ever in the history of Yale.[9] The course content covered topics including:

o The Science of Happiness
o The Practice of Happiness

o   An Authentic Happiness Inventory for pre- and post-course assessments
o   What Stuff Really Increases Happiness
o   Strategies to Reset Our Expectations
o   Putting Strategies into Practice
o   Rewirement—Changing Mindset and Habits

Students were required to practice the following strategies during the class:

o   Savoring
o   Gratitude—daily journal and making phone calls
o   Kindness
o   Meditation
o   Exercise and sleep
o   Goal setting
o   Optimism
o   Understanding "time affluence" compared to "money affluence"

A free, short version of the course is now available on Coursera. com, under the title "The Science of Well-Being."

Another very popular course on this subject is "A Life of Happiness and Fulfillment" by Dr. Rajagopal Raghunathan, professor at the McCombs School of Business, The University of Texas at Austin. This course, started in 2015, is also offered on Coursera.com through the Indian School of Business, Hyderabad, India.[10]

A version of Dr. Raj's course for the business community is titled "Happier Employees and Return on Investment." His 2016 book *If You're So Smart, Why Aren't You Happy* was published by the Penguin division of Random House.

It was Harvard University which got the ball rolling with introducing positive psychology classes to undergraduates. In

1999, the late Phillip J. Stone started a course and had 20 students enrolled.[11]

One of his doctoral graduates took over the course upon his death in 2006 at age 69. Dr. Tal Ben-Shahar named the course "Positive Psychology: On How to be Happier." The course quickly became the most popular course on the Harvard undergraduate campus.

Dr. Ben-Shahar introduced a second course a year later titled "The Psychology of Leadership," which became the third most popular course on campus. His books include *Happier: Learn the Secrets to Daily Joy and Lasting Fulfillment*, and *The Pursuit of Perfect: How to Stop Chasing Perfection and Start Living a Richer, Happier Life.*[12]

I admire Dr. Ben-Shahar very much because of his passion for teaching and writing. As such, he knows he won't make tenure at Harvard. He does not enjoy research, though it is required of tenured faculty. In 2020, he returned to his homeland of Israel to combine closeness to family and opportunities to teach and write—major parts of his personal formula for happiness. An article tells the story of his falling in love at age seven with a six-year-old girl. Many years later, they were married.[13]

Harvard Business School also offers a course on happiness. "Leadership and Happiness" by Arthur C. Brooks. Brooks launched a column in a newspaper, *The Atlantic,* on April 9, 2020. The title of his column is "How to Build a Life."[14]

****

The brief overview of Positive Psychology and happiness given above leads me to believe the next 25 years will see a huge surge in courses on this topic at colleges and universities worldwide. Even community colleges and high schools will start offering practical courses based on the principles being established by the many centers for research on positive psychology.

As I review my life, I see how the concepts and principles of this new approach to helping people thrive could have made a significant difference. Harsh discipline and religious fanaticism rooted my struggles toward self-realization. The use of physical punishment, angry putdowns, and shaming were common parenting techniques. Believing one set of religious beliefs was superior to all others was not conducive to building relationships with those—including relatives—who were not part of the same religious group. I fully understand and accept that our parents and their peers did what they thought was best, given their educational levels, and how they were treated and taught.

A sense of always striving for—but never attaining—perfection, a sense of sinning for simple things like drinking coffee, a strong obligation to aim for a career to please your parents when you are deeply convicted your enjoyment lay elsewhere, and a warped understanding of the importance of earning money—all contributed to my delay in finding satisfaction in my life.

Maybe, positive psychology therapy would have shortened the years to experience the peace and joy of understanding who I am, and why I am here at this time.

When I began to write this chapter, my wife and I took two happiness-related assessments: The *Satisfaction with Life Scale*, and the *Flourishing Scale*. Interestingly enough, my wife scored higher than I did on both—by close to ten points.

That finding triggered an enjoyable conversation on reviewing our 50 years together.

"How can you score this high when five years ago you had major surgery, radiation, and chemotherapy for stage 4 cancer? And since then, you have this autoimmune condition that leaves one leg swollen to about twice the size of the other, and have to be on coumadin and hydroxychloroquine? Over the past two years, you have been hospitalized three times for septicemia, and now manage your periodic outbreaks by keeping two sets of antibiotics on hand at all times."

Her answer boosted my ego and my immediate joy.

> "TIME FLIES FASTEST ON HAPPY WINGS."
> —CAROL BACCHUS

"I have experienced and achieved the vast majority of what I dreamed about as a teenager." Then she added, "time flies fastest on happy wings."

Let's end this chapter with the Flourishing Scale as created, validated, and used in research by Dr. Happiness.

The FLOURISHING SCALE
©Copyright by Ed Diener and Robert Biswas-Diener, January 2009 (Used with permission)

Below are eight statements with which you may agree or disagree. Using the 1–7 scale, indicate your agreement with each item by placing a rating response on the space in front of each statement.

- o 7—Strongly agree
- o 6—Agree
- o 5—Slightly agree
- o 4—Neither agree nor disagree
- o 3—Slightly disagree
- o 2—Disagree
- o 1—Strongly disagree

— I lead a purposeful and meaningful life.
— My social relationships are supportive and rewarding.
— I am engaged and interested in my daily activities.

— I actively contribute to the happiness and well-being of others.
— I am competent and capable in the activities that are important to me.
— I am a good person and live a good life.
— I am optimistic about my future.
— People respect me.

Scoring:
Add the responses, varying from one to seven, for all eight items. The possible range of scores is from 8 (lowest possible) to 56 (highest possible). A high score represents a person with many psychological resources and strengths.

****

Dr. George Vaillant, who directed the Harvard University project "Study of Adult Development" for 32 years, is famous for these two cryptic summary conclusions:[16, 17]

o "Happiness is love, full stop."
o "Happiness is only the cart. The horse is love."

Intuition was not the source of these statements. They were not sudden flights of inspiration, nor the products of philosophical discussions among the world's leading thinkers. Instead, they were summary conclusions from data analysis of the life histories of the 268 Harvard University male graduates from the classes of 1939 through 1944. The study is still ongoing under the directorship of Dr. Robert Waldinger at Massachusetts General Hospital. The lives and medical histories of the "Harvard Cohort" have been compared with the "Boston Cohort," a group of 456 men from the surrounding Boston area, recruited between 1940 and 1945. As participants in the study age and reach the end of their lives, the study will continue with their children.

One other impactful conclusion from this—the longest study of human growth and development ever done—is that change is always possible.

****

There are four other items I would like to point out as you contemplate your personal pursuit of happiness:

1. "World Happiness Day" also called the "International Day of Happiness" is March 20.[18]
2. In January, 2019, the Pew Research Center released a comprehensive study titled: "Religion's Relationship to Happiness, Civic Engagement and Health Around the World."[19] The data supports the concept that religion can promote happiness.
3. The "World Happiness Report" has been issued each year since 2012.[20] The USA has never made the top ten in this rating of over 150 countries. In the 2020 report, Finland is #1, and the USA is #18.
4. Dr. David Blanchflower, an economist at Dartmouth College, showed that happiness over the lifespan follows a U-shaped curve. The low point of the curve occurs during the fourth decade of life—the time of the common mid-life crisis. After that, happiness rises to its highest levels.[21]

After you have reflected on what this chapter covers, you will have some ideas of things you want to include in your book— stories from your life experiences and personal philosophy. Or possibly, things you want to start incorporating into your "pursuit of happiness."

NOTES FOR YOUR BOOK

PART 2

TEN PRACTICES TO PROMOTE HIGH LEVEL WELLNESS OF BODY AND SOUL

When we do the best we can, we never
know what miracle is wrought in
our life, or in the life of another.

—Helen Keller

5

WATER FOR BODY AND SOUL

There is no remedy for love but to love more.

—Henry David Thoreau

Without water, there is no life on Earth. As far as we understand the processes of life, water is the number one requirement. That is why the search for life in the universe beyond Earth, looks first for signs of water.

Water takes up 71% of the surface area on Earth. In the human body, water is 55–60 % of the total components, depending on the proportion of muscle to fat, gender, and age. Babies have a greater percentage of their body weight as water. Men have a larger percentage of body weight as water compared to women.[1]

Other interesting facts about water:

o Of all the water on Earth, 97.5% is salt water, and 2.5% fresh.
o Of the fresh water, 69% is locked in ice and glaciers, and 30% is underground.

o Of the total water on Earth, only 0.007% is available for human use!

Water is the only naturally occurring substance on Earth that exists in three states (liquid, solid, and gas) at temperatures common to Earth. When water freezes at 32 degrees Fahrenheit, it becomes less dense than its liquid form. Ice floats. If it didn't, aquatic life would be in trouble.

Pure water is tasteless, colorless, and odorless. It is neither acidic nor basic.

Other properties include:

o Cohesiveness—the molecules can stick together even as water flows.
o Adhesiveness—water tends to stick to other substances.
o A high heat index—it absorbs a lot of heat before it gets hot.
o A high surface tension—it is elastic, sticky, and allows for movement in small tubes such as the tiniest of blood vessels, the capillaries.

These properties of water are the result of its molecular structure. The two hydrogen atoms connected to the oxygen atom to form water (H_2O), are arranged in a way to give a net positive charge on the hydrogens, and a net negative charge on the oxygen. This polar separation of charges, and the attraction of one molecule to those close by, make water the special substance it is.

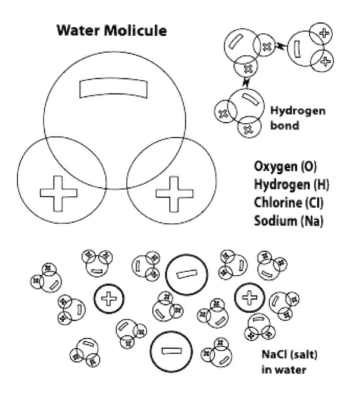

The illustration above summarizes the structural and polar nature of the water molecule, H_2O. In the top, left diagram, the two smaller circles with a + sign are hydrogen atoms, and the large circle with the minus sign is oxygen. The action of water as a solvent for sodium chloride is illustrated at the bottom. The two larger circles with the minus signs are chloride atoms, and the two smaller circles with the + signs are sodium atoms. Water molecules surround each and pull them apart.[2]

WATER FOR THE BODY

Water in the human body serves many functions:

o It is the medium in which all chemical reactions take place. This means without water no chemical reactions take place. And without chemical reactions, there is no life.
o It is a solvent for large molecules. The arrangement of the two hydrogen atoms around the oxygen atom promotes interaction with other molecules to break them into smaller pieces.
o It serves as the transport medium within cells, between cells, and throughout the whole body.
o It functions in excretion by flushing waste as urine and easing the exit of solid waste.
o It helps to maintains normal temperature.
o It serves as a lubricant and cushions organs and joints.
o It helps maintain normal blood pressure by keeping the volume of blood at the right level.

These are the reasons for water being essential to life. The body's water requirement is a daily need estimated by how much water is lost in an average day. This was the basis for the old recommendation of eight 8-oz glasses of water per day—intake to balance output.

There is no specific disease associated with low water intake—only symptoms of dehydration. Death from prolonged water deprivation comes within three–seven days. Because of this, scientists cannot establish a Required Daily Intake. The accepted compromise is to share information on what is called the Adequate Intake.[3]

Adequate Intake is based on what healthy people report. This amounts to 91 ounces per day for the average adult female, and 125 ounces per day for the average adult male.[3] So, eight 8-oz glasses per day, which gives only 64 ounces, may be a minimum, not taking into account other sources of water in food and other liquids.

If we calculate the number of 8-oz glasses for the Adequate Intake, it is approximately 11 for women, and 15 for men. Of course, weather, activity level, and diet will cause wide variations in these amounts. Thirst, weather, and activity level are useful guides to hydration needs. Total water intake from all sources includes pure water in response to thirst, beverages such as coffee and tea or other drinks with meals, and the water content of food.

The simplest estimate of a good hydration level is the frequency of urination and the color of the urine.[4] An average adult needs to empty the bladder about eight times in 24 hours. The urine color varies from clear or light yellow (good hydration), to dark yellow to brown (poor hydration). Of course, diet and vitamin supplements easily influence color.

To summarize water needs for the body:

o About 60% of our body weight is water.
o Without water there is no chemistry to maintain life.
o An average adult female needs 64–90 ounces of water per day from all sources.
o An average adult male needs 64–125 ounces of water per day from all sources.
o Urine color is an acceptable estimate of hydration state.

****

The availability of clean drinking water is a problem for many people worldwide. The World Health Organization estimates:[5]

o In 2017, 71% of the global population (5.3 billion people) used a safely managed drinking-water service—one located on premises, available when needed, and free from contamination. This means 2.2 billion people did not.

o   785 million people lack even a basic drinking-water service, including 144 million people dependent on surface water.

o   Globally, at least two billion people use a drinking water source contaminated with feces.

o   Contaminated water can transmit diseases such as diarrhea, cholera, dysentery, typhoid, and polio. Contaminated drinking water is estimated to cause 485,000 diarrheal deaths each year.

o   By 2025, half of the world's population will be living in water-stressed areas.

o   In the least developed countries, 22% of health care facilities have no water service, 21% no sanitation service, and 22% no waste management service.

GLOBALLY, AT LEAST TWO BILLION PEOPLE USE A DRINKING WATER SOURCE CONTAMINATED WITH FECES.

******

WATER FOR THE SOUL

From the properties and the functions of water in the human body, we can draw some analogies about "spiritual water."

Religion and philosophy allow us to extrapolate from the physical to the spiritual. Group discussions with great diversity in religious and philosophical beliefs raise these spiritual symbolisms and functions of water:

o   Cleansing, purification, and rebirth
o   Thirst satisfaction—fulfills longings for ultimate satisfaction with existential questions
o   Solvent function—dissolves discord and leads to acceptance of differences
o   Promotes cohesiveness—group, family, and as part of all humanity
o   High heat absorption before boiling point—absorbs lots of provocation before hot-tempered outbursts

The various world religions address these applications through each founder's teachings. Let's do a bullet-point summary of the major religions.[6, 7]

o   Christianity—Jesus is the water of life, cleansing from sin, and giver of eternal life; water immersion symbolic of new life.
o   Islam—cleansing, purification, ablutions should be done before prayer and worship.
o   Hinduism—cleansing especially from the holy waters of the sacred rivers such as the Ganges and Yamuna; a pilgrimage of Kumbh Mela every 12 years (next one in 2025); a dip in the holy waters cleanses the life of all sins.
o   Buddhism—water is transformative and life-giving. It represents purity, clarity, and calmness, and symbolizes the Buddha's teachings.
o   Judaism—cleansing, ablution, and purification are rituals in various services.

RECOMMENDED PRACTICE

Establish a daily habit of drinking water as the first thing to enter the body on awakening from sleep. Meditate on the spiritual significance of water according to your belief system.

Satisfy the thirst as dictated by the level of activity and weather throughout the day. Water before or during meals helps ensure the body is adequately hydrated.

Think about some quality of water that relates to how you can be helpful to others during the day. Are you a lubricant for discord? Does your presence generate calmness, cohesiveness, purification, clarity, and transformation?

****

Water Stories—Growing Up in Richland Park, St. Vincent, in the 1950s

Our main source of water was the river that flowed along the east side of the village. For drinking water, we would go to the river and scoop up water into a five-gallon bucket and put it on our heads to walk the half-mile back home.

For laundering clothes, we would take the clothes to the river and rub and beat them on the stones, wash, rinse, and spread out to dry in the sunlight, then carry them back home in large baskets on our heads.

Looking back, I wonder how we survived without major outbreaks of water-borne diseases. The river was open to all at many different points. Those living upstream would wash clothes, bathe, and have animals drink and deposit wastes. At the same time, those downstream could be collecting drinking water, washing clothes, and bathing. There were occasions when human feces went floating by from upstream, even while others downstream were bathing.

The other source of water close to our house was a spring in "Bottom Village." The village was a hilly place and water collected to form a spring. The wonder of it all is everybody had outhouses over pits about six to eight feet deep. How did water at the bottom of the hilly landscape become purified enough for drinking? I do not recall any major outbreak of cholera or another water-borne disease.

It was a great sign of progress to go back home 20 years later and see a controlled water system piped through the village, with flush toilets inside the homes!

****

The following quote from philosopher Bertrand Russell will end this chapter with a more pleasant thought.

> "An individual human existence should be like a river—small at first, narrowly contained within its banks, and rushing passionately past rocks and over waterfalls. Gradually, the river grows wider, the banks recede, the waters flow more quietly, and in the end, without any visible break, they become merged in the sea, and painlessly lose their individual being."[8]

NOTES FOR YOUR BOOK

6

DNA FOR BODY AND SOUL

I don't want to live. I want to love first, and live
incidentally. Nobody has ever measured, not even poets,
how much the heart can hold.

—Zelda Fitzgerald

What is DNA? The abbreviation means De-oxy-ribo-Nucleic Acid. This is the molecule that carries our genes—the code for what makes us who we are.

There is an abundance of information available to the public on trusted websites, so it is unnecessary to say a lot about DNA in this short overview. DNA is referred to as the genetic material or molecule, and the word "genome" is used to refer to all the genetic material in a given organism.

Before I get to the applications to the health of body and soul, here are a few key facts:[1, 2]

o   If all the DNA in a single cell is laid out end-to-end in a straight line, it would measure six feet long and consist of a six billion letter code.

o   The molecule and its associated proteins were first isolated in 1869 by Frederich Miescher, a Swiss biochemist, who named it "nuclein."

o   The molecular structure of DNA was established in 1953 by James Watson, Rosalind Franklin, and Francis Crick, along with their team of researchers using x-ray diffraction and ball-and-stick models.

o   Genes carry information to make proteins which are responsible for the function and appearance of traits.

o   Between the years 1950 and 2003, college professors taught that humans have 100,000 genes. The prevailing belief was one gene made only one protein, and the estimated number of proteins was 100,000! In 2003, the Human Genome Project was completed and found only 20,000–25,000 genes in the human genome.

The double-stranded structure of DNA is also referred to as a "double-helix" made up of a sugar-phosphate backbone, with interconnecting strands of four nitrogen-based molecules: adenine (A), which pairs with thymine (T), and cytosine (C), which pairs with guanine (G).

The illustrations below show the double-stranded nature with the base pairings A–T and C–G. The ball-and-stick model gives a visual representation of the arrangement of the molecules in a portion of DNA

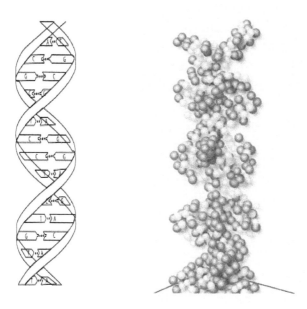

A gene is a segment of the DNA molecule with the code to produce a protein. When it is time to make a protein, that segment of DNA unwinds and gets transcribed into a single-stranded messenger RNA (Ribo-Nucleic Acid). The mRNA leaves the nucleus and goes out into the cytoplasm, where the code translates into the correct protein.

Proteins are made of amino acids. The code in mRNA contains information that says how many of each type of amino acid and in what order. The released protein then goes to where it is needed to carry out its function. (The technology of how to use mRNA to produce a vaccine is what enabled scientists to mount the rapid response to the 2020–2021 worldwide viral threat.)

Proteins control all physical qualities (skin color, height, shape, and color of body parts), and all metabolic functions (energy producing pathways and hormone actions).

With this brief overview, let's consider health effects, then spiritual applications.

If DNA is damaged, the code to make a specific protein is disrupted. The consequence of this disruption is the protein is either not created or is produced with missing parts so it cannot perform its normal function. DNA can be damaged by radiation, and chemicals.

Genetic errors include missing whole or parts of a DNA molecule, extra DNA, or changes in the code which are referred to as mutations. The results of these errors are genetic diseases such as Down Syndrome (extra DNA), and some forms of breast cancer (mutation in a specific gene).

Today, DNA technology has progressed so that gene replacement is possible. It is routine to clone animals, select human embryos with specific traits, and create new varieties of fruits and vegetables to increase yield and quality.[3]

Several well-known diseases are passed on from one generation to the next via the genes. Examples include cystic fibrosis, hemophilia, and sickle cell disease.[4]

One source of potential damage for DNA is a set of unstable molecules called free radicals. Free radicals are produced naturally in the body during the normal process of extracting energy from food. Since free radicals are unstable, they seek to steal electrons from nearby molecules such as DNA. This can cause mutations in DNA and may lead to cancer.[5]

Antioxidants are molecules that neutralize free radicals. The body has naturally occurring antioxidants but over the last 20 years a multi-billion-dollar industry in marketing supplements has popularized the use of several common antioxidants. These include vitamins A, C, and E, beta carotene, lycopene from tomatoes, and lutein.

The current consensus of scientific opinion is that if we have a diet which includes a variety of colored plant material daily, supplementation with manufactured antioxidants is not necessary.[6]

In fact, there is evidence that free radicals play a beneficial role in stimulating our natural immune defenses, and overloading the body with antioxidants may not be the preventive measure it was once thought to be.[7]

RECOMMENDATION:

For the protection of our DNA, we need antioxidants. The body of current evidence says we can get an adequate supply from various plant sources in the diet. Supplementation is not necessary unless the diet is deficient in plant material. One good maxim is, "Aim to eat a rainbow every day."

****

SPIRITUAL DNA:

The application here will focus on a Christian extrapolation from physical DNA. Other belief systems may make similar extrapolations. It makes for a pleasant exchange of ideas to see how different belief systems apply these analogies.

> WE ARE HARDWIRED TO LOVE; IT IS IN THE FIRST STRAND OF OUR SPIRITUAL DNA.

- o Our spiritual DNA is double stranded like our physical DNA. The first strand is the imprint of God's character at creation. Genesis 1:27 tells us, God created human beings in his own image. The Bible also tells us God is love. So, we are hardwired to love; it is in the first strand of our spiritual DNA.
- o The second strand of spiritual DNA is the writing of God's law on the heart and mind in the "new covenant." Hebrews 8:10 tells us, "But this is the new covenant I

will make with the people of Israel on that day, says the Lord. I will put my laws in their minds, and I will write them on their hearts. I will be their God, and they will be my people."

o The product of this spiritual genetic code (spiritual proteins?) is the fruit of the Spirit: love, joy, peace, longsuffering, kindness, goodness, faithfulness, gentleness, and self-control (Galatians 5:22).

o Protection of spiritual DNA from free radical damage includes giving reasons for your beliefs, being open to discussing other peoples' beliefs in an honest, friendly exploration of differences, and purposefully cultivating the qualities that reflect God's character in dealing with others—intentionally living the fruit of the Spirit.

RECOMMENDED PRACTICE

If your belief system is Christian, like mine, then reading Scripture, meditating on God's nature, and His role in the universe will protect the spiritual DNA. Beliefs and teachings are of no value if they do not impact our dealings with others in positive, uplifting, and practically helpful ways.

People with other belief systems expect the same outcome. It is not the main point whether or not an analogy from physical DNA to spiritual DNA is possible. The main point is how our belief systems cause us to treat one another.

Before I ask you to make notes of ideas or thoughts for your book, here are my reflections on DNA from my life:

o It is very scary to take courses in genetics and embryology while your wife is pregnant. When you have to study all that can go wrong during the changes from a single cell to a fully formed human being, you wonder how things go right so often.

o   I believe my nasty temper is part of my genetic inheritance. It has been a major challenge in my life when dealing with family and others.

o   The methods used by my parents for discipline influenced my early disciplinary methods with my children. My awakening came during an angry confrontation with my 13-year-old son, when I realized he was stronger than me, and he had inherited my hot temper! (He was stubborn and strong-willed from day one.) Since then, we have had a smooth journey. At 48 years of age, he is one of my best friends. It was one of my dreams as a teenager to have a son with whom I could develop a close, loving relationship. Life has blessed me with two sons! Nowadays, we carry on an almost daily text or phone chat, focused on what we are doing for our personal wellness, and plans for vacations together.

NOTES FOR YOUR BOOK

7

ENERGY AND OXYGEN FOR BODY AND SOUL

The brain may take advice, but not the heart, and love,
having no geography, knows no boundaries.

—Truman Capote

The sun, which is essentially a big ball of hydrogen, is the source of all the energy that makes life possible on Earth. It is so large that the core is very dense, and nuclear fusion takes place. Hydrogen atoms are fused to become helium in a continuous cycle.

The vast amount of energy produced from nuclear fusion then leaks to the outer layers and escapes from the outermost layer, the photosphere—the visible surface. (The corona is the outermost layer of the sun's atmosphere.) The energy that travels to Earth consists of radio waves, microwaves, infrared, visible, and ultraviolet waves. This is known as the electromagnetic spectrum.[1]

Of all the planets in the solar system, only Earth is at the proper distance from the sun to be able to support life as we know it. The position of Earth is referred to as "The Habitable Zone," or "The Goldilocks Zone."[2]

In this habitable zone, the atmosphere's composition allows for the right amount of energy from the sun to pass through, to maintain a temperature on the planet at which water can remain as a liquid. None of the other planets in the solar system has this combination of conditions.

Of all the energy released from the sun, it is estimated that one one-billionth reaches Earth. More than 99% of that warms the atmosphere and the earth itself, creates the weather and gets reflected into space.[3]

Less than one percent of the sun's energy that reaches Earth gets trapped by green plants (also algae and some bacteria) and becomes the energy that sustains all living things. The process of photosynthesis uses sunlight to trap carbon dioxide and water to form a sugar molecule called glucose. Glucose and similar sugars form all other carbohydrates.

When animals eat plants first-hand or second-hand, they get the energy to power the metabolic processes that sustain life. The process to extract energy from glucose is called cellular respiration.

The equations can be simplified as follows:

Photosynthesis (P) = Carbon dioxide + water + sunlight → *glucose + oxygen*

Cellular Respiration (CR) = glucose + oxygen → *energy (ATP) + carbon dioxide + water*

The two processes are dependent on each other. P traps carbon using sunlight and releases oxygen. CR needs oxygen to release the energy in glucose and gives off carbon dioxide. P uses carbon dioxide to repeat the cycle to make more glucose.

The energy produced in CR is trapped in the form of ATP (Adenosine Tri-Phosphate).

This molecule is referred to as "the energy currency of the cell." Here's an illustration of the structure of ATP.

*From right to left: adenine, ribose,
three phosphate groups.*

The terminal phosphate group is called a high energy phosphate, and releases energy to power metabolic reactions. The key point from this discussion is: energy from the sun becomes part of all life as ATP. Without the sun, there is no life on Earth— or more correctly, no Earth.

ROLE OF OXYGEN[4]

Most of the ATP production from glucose occur in the mitochondria—little organelles known as "the powerhouses of the cell."

Energy is trapped in the glucose molecule when six carbon atoms join together, and the hydrogen and oxygen atoms attach during photosynthesis. To extract this energy and make ATP, the hydrogen atoms are plucked off, and the carbon atoms are dislodged from one another. This breaking of chemical bonds releases energy that is captured as ATP.

The chemical reactions that release this energy is an orderly metabolic process. Several enzymes, arranged in an exact sequence on the mitochondria's inner membrane, drive the process of energy extraction. A cascade of electrons and hydrogen ions flows down this pathway to generate ATP.

At the end of the electron transport chain, the free electrons and the free hydrogen and carbon atoms are collected by oxygen to form water and carbon dioxide. Without oxygen, this process stops.

Of course, we need to get oxygen from the atmosphere. We also need to get rid of excess carbon dioxide. This is the function of the lungs—intake of a fresh supply of oxygen, and exhaling carbon dioxide. Oxygen from the lungs then enters the bloodstream, where most of it attaches to hemoglobin. Hemoglobin unloads oxygen in the small blood vessels. The oxygen diffuses across the tissue space, across the cell membranes, and gets into the mitochondria.

ENERGY NEEDS OF THE HUMAN BODY

Energy is measured in kilocalories. One kilocalorie is the amount of energy it takes to raise the temperature of 1000 milliliters of water by one degree centigrade at sea level. This is represented by a capital C and used to measure food energy.

The basal metabolic rate (BMR) is the required number of Calories to sustain function when the body is in a quiet, awake state after a 12-hour fast. This varies by size and age. There are several calculators available, based on formulas derived from experiments.

BMR is not useful unless you plan to lose or gain weight. The formula is adjustable for an increase or a decrease of activity and calorie intake. One of the best calculators available—The Body Weight Planner—is on the website of the National Institute of Diabetes, Digestive, and Kidney Disease.[5]

The balancing of the intake of calories with output is key to maintaining healthy energy levels. Excess calories get stored as fat. Insufficient calories put key vital organs such as heart and skeletal muscle at risk for weakness and damage.

****

SPIRITUAL ATP

One of the joys of teaching with academic freedom is to throw out ideas for students to see if they can improve a concept. Here are some spiritual lessons that relate to energy from the sun, and the role of ATP. They have been refined with student input over several years.

o   Just as without the sun there cannot be life on earth, without Christ there would be no Christianity. The question becomes, do Christians make a positive difference in the world?

o   One passage of Old Testament Scripture says: "But to you who fear My name, The Sun of Righteousness will rise with healing in his wings. And you will go free, leaping with joy like calves let out to pasture" (Malachi 4:2). Does Christianity generate righteous dealings among humans?

o   Just as energy from the sun sustains life on Earth, the spiritual life-sustaining energy for a Christian comes through the belief that Christ is who He said He is.

o   Spiritual ATP is the righteousness of Christ. Just as humans cannot live without continuous ATP production, a Christian cannot functionally exist without Christ's righteousness. The spiritual ATP must continuously bathe the lives of Christians with enthusiasm to live out the character of Christ.

At this point in class discussions, I mostly receive agreements with these ideas. My devout Muslim students, whom I've had the pleasure of having in classes for my last four years of teaching, usually add the Prophet Muhammad's role, and passages from the Quran to share their thoughts.

SPIRITUAL OXYGEN

I had to memorize this quote in elementary school: "Prayer is the breath of the soul." With that background, my mind had to connect breathing to the main purpose of breathing—to get oxygen to cells and expel carbon dioxide.

So, to summarize my spiritual applications from energy and oxygen in the lives of Christians:

o   Christ is the source of all energy, inspiration, and desire for zestful living (sun).
o   The righteousness and character of Christ provide motivation for living a good life (ATP).
o   Prayer—communication with the Higher Power in which an individual believes—is like breathing to receive the agent (oxygen) to harvest ATP for the soul.

In discussion groups, each person with a different belief system gets a chance to explain how these ideas may find applications within their practices.

******

APPLICATIONS FOR PHYSICAL HEALTH

The benefits of sunlight include the following:[6]

o   It increases vitamin D production.
o   It enhances immune system modulation.
o   It regulates serotonin and melatonin levels. Serotonin is a brain chemical that elevates mood. Exposure to sunlight boosts its production. Serotonin is a precursor of melatonin. When serotonin levels rise in daylight,

melatonin levels are increased earlier in the dark. This results in better sleep.

o   Sunlight increases endorphin levels and reduces pain.

Recommendation: if possible, get adequate sun exposure daily appropriate for your skin type and geographic location; darker skin tones require longer exposure. Be knowledgeable about skin cancer risks from over exposure to the UV rays of the sun. The American Cancer Society provides good guidance on these risks.[7]

> SUNLIGHT INCREASES ENDORPHIN LEVELS AND REDUCES PAIN.

OXYGENATION

The common habit of shallow breathing may rob the body of adequate amounts of oxygen. In shallow breathing, the movement of the diaphragm is restricted. The small blood vessels at the base of the lungs do not get exposed to the air/blood interphase. The blood picks up less oxygen.[8]

Recommendation: Practice deep-breathing regularly. (A protocol is given in Appendix I.)

APPLICATIONS FOR SPIRITUAL HEALTH

According to your belief system,

o   Maintain daily exposure to what is your most inspirational example of how to live with love for everyone with whom you interact.

o   Have prayer and communication with whom you believe is the greatest power in the universe.

The story that comes to mind here is about overexposure to the sun. My wife is a white woman from Illinois. I'm an Indian guy from the Caribbean. When we go to the beach, I often use little or no sunscreen. During one summer beach trip, she forgot to lather with sunscreen, and, oh, the blisters and pain from both legs! For several days, she had to scoot up and down the stairs on her bum since she couldn't walk upright. Since then, she hasn't forgotten to put on sunscreen whenever we spend time outdoors.

What stories, questions, and comments might this chapter have stirred in your mind?

NOTES FOR YOUR BOOK

_____

_____

_____

_____

_____

_____

_____

_____

_____

_____

_____

_____

_____

_____

_____

_____

_____

_____

_____

_____

_____

8

NUTRITION FOR BODY AND SOUL

Love is a fruit in season at all times,
and within reach of every hand.

—Mother Teresa

My freshmen college students in "Fitness and Wellness" frequently asked me: "Which is more important—good nutrition, exercise, or stress management?'

Well, they are all very important. Are you looking to choose one over the others? They are important for different effects on health. If I were to choose one to emphasize, I would pay more attention to managing stress than to foods I consume, providing I have enough to eat. I hate to go hungry! I see exercise as play, so it's easy to work in exercise.

FOOD FOR THE BODY

The principles of healthy nutrition are very well established and well publicized. The difficulty is getting the public to make healthy choices based on science. It seems when science conflicts with taste and habits, science loses most of the time.

For our purposes in this chapter, I will restate the best research-based information and give references for more details. Providing recommendations for what works is the most a teacher or writer can do. The actions required to accomplish the goals are up to the individual.

The extensive, five-year review of the science-based recommendations for the dietary guidelines for Americans has been completed. The final publication of the 2020–2025 Dietary Guidelines was released in December, 2020.[1] Since these guidelines are based on studies and reviews of the world-wide scientific literature, the general principles apply to the rest of the world.

The 2015–2020 Guidelines contain the current, major recommendations for diet and health. The 2020–2025 recommendations contain specific adjustments to the current guidelines across the lifespan. They also show the relationships between dietary practices and specific disease/health outcomes.

The highlights below are from the 2015–2020 Guidelines. The five overarching principles as given in the Executive Summary are:

1. Follow a healthy eating pattern across the lifespan. All food and beverage choices matter. Choose a healthy eating pattern at an appropriate calorie level to help achieve and maintain a healthy body weight, support nutrient needs, and reduce chronic disease risks.
2. Focus on variety, nutrient density, and amount. To meet nutrient needs within calorie limits, choose a variety of nutrient-dense foods across and within all food groups in recommended amounts.
3. Establish an eating pattern low in added sugars, saturated fats, and sodium. Cut back on foods and beverages higher

in these components to amounts that fit within healthy eating patterns.

4. Shift to healthier food and beverage choices. Choose nutrient-dense foods and beverages across and within all food groups in place of less healthy choices. Consider cultural and personal preferences to make these shifts easier to accomplish and maintain.

5. Support healthy eating patterns for all. Everyone has a role in helping to create and support healthy eating patterns in multiple settings, from home to school to work to communities.

"Eating pattern" is the designation for the composition of the diet, meaning what people customarily eat. A healthy eating pattern includes:

o A variety of vegetables from all of the subgroups—dark green, red and orange, legumes (beans and peas), starchy, and other
o Fruits, especially fresh, whole fruits, not canned
o Grains, at least half of which are whole grains
o Fat-free or low-fat dairy, including milk, yogurt, cheese, and/or fortified soy beverages
o A variety of protein foods, including seafood, lean meats and poultry, eggs, legumes, nuts, seeds, and soy products
o Oils

A healthy eating pattern limits saturated and trans fats, added sugars and sodium.

o Consume less than ten percent of calories per day from added sugar.
o Consume less than ten percent of calories per day from saturated fat.

- o Consume less than 2,300 milligrams (mg) per day of sodium.
- o Consume alcohol in moderation—up to one drink per day for women and up to two drinks per day for men—and only by adults of legal drinking age.

Recent surveys of populations who have the greatest longevity show:

- o A plant-based diet affords the greatest health benefits.
- o Humans can get all their nutrient needs on a vegetarian or vegan diet. This includes complete protein, vitamin B12, and all trace elements.
- o The most popular eating pattern is the Mediterranean diet.
- o Along with the positive benefits of increased fiber, a plant-based diet provides all needed vitamins and antioxidants. Supplementation with manufactured pills is not necessary for otherwise healthy individuals.

EATING PATTERNS IN THE "BLUE ZONES:"

In 2016, the American Journal of Lifestyle Medicine released a summary of the findings among populations designated "Blue Zones."[2] This was the result of the National Geographic search to find the secrets of longevity among communities where people routinely lived healthy lives well into their 90s and over 100 years.

Five places around the world qualified: Okinawa, Japan; Sardinia, Italy; Loma Linda, CA; Nicoya, Costa Rica; and Ikaria, Greece. The summary is worth reading. It puts nutrition as only one factor among nine that contribute to healthy, long, and happy lives.

What are the eating patterns for these healthiest places on Earth?

Ikaria, Greece: the Mediterranean diet with lots of fruits and vegetables, whole grains, beans, potatoes, olive oil, herbal teas and goats' milk, 5% meats, and 6% fish.

Loma Linda, CA: whole grains, fruits, vegetable, legumes, peas, beans, nuts (five times per week), soy, 10% dairy, and 4% meats.

Sardinia, Italy: whole-grain bread, beans, fruits, vegetables, small amounts of meat (5% of diet), and 26% dairy.

Okinawa, Japan: 67% of the diet is sweet potatoes, stir-fried vegetables, soy (tofu), 12% rice, legumes, 2% fish, meat, or poultry.

Nicoya, Costa Rica: squash, corn, beans, whole grain, fruits, vegetables, 24% dairy, and 5% meat, fish, or poultry.

The commonality is over 80% of the diet is plant-based, with low meat and dairy consumption. The other factors that contribute to the long, happy life include activity, lots of sex, purpose in life, and social interaction.[3]

Several years after the initial reports on these high longevity communities, the National Geographic Society and the National Institute of Aging tested the findings in prospective projects in American cities. The effort was to engage whole communities in lifestyle change, especially healthy eating patterns, and track the results.[3]

> THE COMMONALITY IS OVER 80% OF THE DIET IS PLANT-BASED, WITH LOW MEAT AND DAIRY CONSUMPTION.

Dan Buettner's 2015 book *The Blue Zones Solution: Eating and Living Like the World's Healthiest People* summarizes the plan. It also includes the findings of testing the plan in communities in Minnesota and California. In conjunction with the Dietary Guidelines described above, this book will provide all the healthy eating recommendations needed for a happy, healthy life.

If we have a good sense of trust in what the science says and can see examples of people living long, healthy, happy lives, we can have confidence we are on the right track. This diffuses any anxiety when fad diet after fad diet hits the market. Whether it is for weight loss or overall health, it seems there is a new craze each year.

Recent popular diets include the Paleo Diet and the Ketogenic Diet. Both of these seem to be nutritionally unbalanced. Paleo's emphasis on eating the foods cavemen used to eat, leaves out grains, legumes, and dairy. It recommends only meats, fish, fruits, vegetables, nuts, and seeds. That makes it a high protein, low carb eating pattern.[4]

The Keto Diet is a high fat, high protein, low carbohydrate eating pattern shown to have positive effects on weight loss, and control of type 2 diabetes. Though not recommended as a long-term eating pattern, it may be effective in medically supervised cases.[5]

In summary, a healthy eating pattern over the life span should be a high plant-based diet, low animal products, and whole foods as much as possible. The Blue Zone communities worldwide continue to lead the way for low incidence of chronic diseases, greater longevity, and longer healthy, active years.

****

MINDFUL EATING

One key to healthy eating patterns is to solve the conflict among the physiologic drives of appetite, hunger, cravings, satiety, culture, and scientific knowledge. Early in life, food composition and the balance between hormone signals for hunger and satisfaction set the appetite. We regulate it throughout life, and subject it to conscious control.

Two hormones play a role in regulating hunger and appetite. Ghrelin, primarily produced in the stomach, acts on the brain centers to signal hunger and turn on the appetite.[6] Leptin, produced mainly by fat cells, acts on the brain centers to reduce food intake and increase metabolic rate. Overeating has been shown to produce leptin resistance, thus decreasing energy use and increasing fat tissue.

With these hormonal systems influenced by the genes for obesity in the background, the question is: can humans exercise conscious control over hunger and appetite? This is where the positive psychology of "mindfulness" will give the answer that yes, we can.[7, 8]

Dr. Jon Kabat-Zinn did the original research on mindfulness at the University of Massachusetts Medical School. One of his first practices to learn mindfulness was called "How to Eat a Raisin."[9] (I recall taking individual mini-boxes of raisins to my classroom when we practiced this exercise. We each ate one raisin for the exercise, then had a whole box for an in-class or after-class snack.)

Along with mindfulness for eating, Dr. Kabat-Zinn researched mindfulness-based stress reduction. His definition of mindfulness is: "paying attention in a particular way, on purpose, in the present moment, and non-judgmentally, in the service of self-understanding and wisdom." Currently, most major universities and medical schools have centers for mindfulness, and the practices are incorporated into medical care.

The steps in mindfulness for eating include:

o   paying attention to feelings—hunger, cravings, etc.
o   paying attention to the food items and choices
o   thinking about health benefits and health consequences of the choices
o   deciding to quit eating before stretching the stomach and abdominal muscles.

Part of the control of eating exerted by the Japanese in the Okinawa Blue Zone is repeating a mantra before eating. The old Confucian mantra is: "Hara Hachi Bu," which means "eat until you are 80% full." This prevents overeating in a mindful way.[3]

******

FOOD FOR THE SOUL

All religions and all philosophies will find many similarities in what feeds the soul. So, let's make a list and find what touches us:

- o Scripture—reading, memorizing, and meditating on passages that speak to deep inner convictions, and which stir inspirational thoughts
- o Music—from classical, gospel, and great choir pieces, country and the love songs of the fifties, sixties, and seventies—the music itself, and the lyrics
- o Poetry—from simple rhymes to wandering abstract themes (I can still recite poems we had to memorize in grade school.)
- o Books—from the great writers to Perry Mason novels—stories or expositions that capture the mind and transport us out of this world
- o Meditation, contemplation of life, the universe, and the place of the individual in it
- o Beautiful scenery in natural settings

These things engender thought, inspire creative ideas, and when engaged fully, transport the mind to transcendental places.

NOTES FOR YOUR BOOK

_____

_____

_____

_____

_____

_____

_____

_____

_____

_____

_____

_____

_____

_____

_____

_____

_____

_____

_____

_____

_____

_____

9
STRESS ADAPTATION FOR BODY AND SOUL

The course of true love never did run smooth.

—William Shakespeare

Two short stories come to mind as I begin this chapter. The first is about taking a graduate level stress management course in the Department of Health Education at the University of Maryland, then teaching an undergraduate course in stress management at Washington Adventist University. The second story is about my personal use of a relaxation technique to get off strong medications—Librium and tincture of belladonna alkaloids.

With a graduate level course, you have to cover everything—background history, the research in stress mechanisms, the health consequences of stress, and techniques or skills to reduce stress, become resistant to stress, or avoid stress. So, we'd start with the "father of stress physiology research," Hans Selye (1907–1982).[1]

Selye, a Hungarian-Canadian endocrinologist, did his landmark work at McGill University and the University of Montreal. He was likely driven by the stresses in his own life.

He was married three times. He stayed in the second, unhappy marriage for 28 years so that his four children could have a stable home till they became independent. Later, he married his lab assistant. His prolific work resulted in over 1500 scientific papers, and 40 books.[2]

From Selye, we got two simple phrases that summarized stress physiology: "the syndrome of just being sick," and "the general adaptation syndrome." In his research he identified the hypothalamus, the pituitary, and the adrenal glands as the axis of the stress response.

In the graduate course, the laboratory exercises challenged my conservative, western, Judeo-Christian background and beliefs. We were learning meditation and yoga. I was concerned about mind-manipulating techniques that may lead to others being able to control my thoughts.

When I started teaching my undergraduate course in stress management, I would bring all the material from that graduate course and introduce mindfulness, meditation, relaxation, and yoga. Knowing the conservative stance of the institution I worked for, I had to disguise my yoga positions as "stretching." It was gratifying that after eight years in that department, students were comfortable with demonstrating "downward dog" and other yoga positions without any fear of censorship.

For each successive year of teaching that undergraduate course, I reduced the amount of research material and increased the time spent with the practices. Learning what works was priority to learning the history and research physiology behind the concepts.

In this chapter, I'll give a brief introduction to stress adaptation, and spend most time on techniques that have been shown to work.

The technique that I have tested in my own dealings with stress is the relaxation response as researched and established by Herbert Benson, MD, at Harvard University.[3] It worked for me.

****

My Encounter with the Effects of Stress

As a father of three, I tried to live up to my life's ideals which included having my wife stay at home to care for the children while I worked full-time. I was still applying to medical schools in the effort to fulfill my mother's dream of having a doctor in the family. At the same time, I was completing a post-doctoral fellowship in research physiology at the University of Virginia and being faithful to my church's teachings on paying tithes and being an active member.

Then, I blew it wide open with my impulsive resignation from my first post-graduate job. We lost two houses in one year, spent a few months as a homeless family, and eventually filed for bankruptcy.

Stress-related symptoms including spastic colon syndrome and restless sleep sent me to the doctor's office. In the early 1980s, the stress response was not considered in dealing with symptoms where there was no definite disease. If the blood analyses, GI x-rays, and barium enemas didn't show any abnormalities, it was standard practice to treat the symptoms.

My prescription was for a tranquilizer, Librium, and tincture of belladonna alkaloids (a smooth muscle poison) to quiet the spastic colon. I remained on these for about two years without much reduction of symptoms.

During the 1985–86 school year, I learned about the Society for Behavioral Medicine in my coursework at the University of Maryland and decided to attend the annual meeting. The president of the society that year was Dr. Herbert Benson, and the relaxation response was a major feature.

I learned the process to trigger the relaxation response and practiced it faithfully for about three months. My symptoms disappeared, and I got off the Librium and belladonna alkaloids.

Now, this is just an anecdote—not research. Other factors in my life had changed by then. One major factor was a job with the heart surgeons at Washington Hospital Center making three times the salary at the job I had impulsively quit. Of course, teaching the relaxation response became a standard part of all my health courses.

******

SUMMARY OF STRESS PHYSIOLOGY

Three major concepts from Hans Selye were:[4, 5]

1. A definition of stress. He defined stress as: "the excess wear and tear on the body." This indicates that, throughout life, wear and tear are unavoidable. Some heightened demand on the body is good for increased productivity. Beyond that, the body starts to break down and lose function when the wear and tear exceed countermeasures to preserve homeostasis.

2. A general summary for sickness. He coined the term "the syndrome of just being sick" to refer to the general signs and symptoms that seem to be common to all illnesses. Apart from the main disease, there is a generalized reduction in function that accompanies all disease processes.

3. A general summary of dealing with stress. The "general adaptation syndrome" refers to the body's response to excess wear and tear. Through many basic physiology experiments, Selye established that the hypothalamus in the brain communicates with the pituitary gland, which sends messages to all other glands around the body, with strongest effects on the adrenal glands. This orchestrates the stress response in three stages: the alarm reaction, the resistance stage, and the exhaustion stage.

Further research into stress physiology linked the cerebral cortex to the act of perceiving threats, then triggering the hypothalamus to respond. This link is now referred to as the cortico-hypothalamic-pituitary-adrenal axis.[6] For wellness promotion, we must reduce all this information into simpler language for use in everyday health strategies.[7]

The major events of the stress response are:[8]

o Conscious perception of threats generates nerve impulses from the cortex to the hypothalamus and amygdala. The "flight-or-fight" response gets triggered.

o The hypothalamus releases several hormones and neurotransmitters that trigger the pituitary gland.

o The pituitary gland—the master gland—sends activating hormones to the adrenal glands (and others such as thyroids, ovaries, testes, kidneys, and liver).

o The adrenals respond with two chemicals that directly affect the stress adaptation: adrenaline to speed up immediate response and cortisol for more long-term adaptation.

o Cortisol enters the brain and affects chemical manufacture and release. This impacts mood, fear, and motivation. Cortisol also increases blood glucose and suppresses the function of other systems that are not involved in responding to the perceived threat. So, the immune, digestive, and reproductive systems, and growth/healing can be affected.

o Negative health effects of frequent or chronic stress result from frequent surges or prolonged high levels of adrenaline and cortisol.

The above summary explains why ulcers, spastic colon, high blood pressure, heart disease, reproductive problems, and lower immune system function can be stress related. One of the tenets of stress control is each individual may have a specific system most susceptible to the effects of stress. I know from experience that I am a gut responder.

We now know that we need to reduce stress, build resistance to inevitable stress, reduce the effects of stress, and manage stress to mitigate negative health effects.

The illustration below summarizes the pathways of the body's stress adaptation systems.

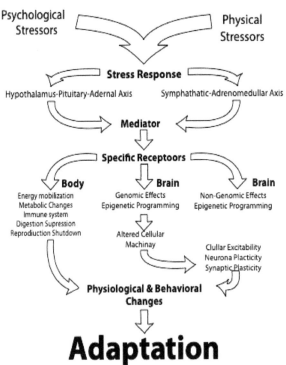

(Used by permission of the authors.)

The diagram shows:

o Physical and psychological stress activate the same pathways.
o The cascade of events starts in the higher information processing centers of the brain—the cortex—then lower centers turn on. Perception and evaluation precede hormonal and nervous responses.
o The hypothalamus-pituitary-adrenal axis triggers hormonal pathways.
o The sympathetic nervous system triggers more short-acting nerve pathways.
o Mediators are hormones or nerve signals.
o Effects in the brain include influence on genes in epigenetic programming—stress from the environment can turn genes on or off.
o All effects then lead to changes in cellular chemical pathways on vulnerable body systems.
o The result is physiological and/or behavioral changes.

SIGNS AND SYMPTOMS OF STRESS

The effects of stress on the body range from mild disturbances in function to chronic disease. These include:[9]

o Sleep disturbances
o GI symptoms such as indigestion, ulcers, spastic colon
o Increased muscle tension
o Fatigue
o Loss of concentration
o Headaches
o Anxiety
o Decreased sexual desire and drive
o Heart palpitations

- o Chronic disease such as type 2 diabetes, obesity, and heart disease
- o Increased susceptibility to colds and upper respiratory infections

TECHNIQUES AND SKILLS TO MANAGE STRESS

- o Good nutrition[10]
  - o A diet similar to those of the Blue Zone communities is linked to reduced anxiety.
  - o A diet with high intake of fruit, vegetables, whole grain, fish, olive oil, low-fat dairy, antioxidants, and low intake of animal foods is associated with a decreased risk of depression.
  - o A diet with a high consumption of red and/or processed meat, refined grains, sweets, high-fat dairy products, butter, potatoes, high-fat gravy, and low intakes of fruits and vegetables is associated with an increased risk of depression."[11]

- o Exercise[12]
  - o Distracts the mind and breaks recurring thoughts.
  - o Stimulates the production of endorphins, which are natural pain killers.
  - o Increases blood flow to the brain and strengthens the heart.
  - o Reduces the production of adrenaline and cortisol.
  - o Reduces anxiety and depression.
  - o Enjoyable activity stimulates neurochemicals in the brain that lifts mood and enhances motivation.

- o Mental and Psychological Skills (More details in Appendix 1)
  - o Savoring—taking time to focus on good things and the enjoyment they bring to your consciousness
  - o Mindfulness—paying attention to *now*
  - o Gratitude—beyond the everyday *thank you*
  - o Forgiving—as needed
  - o Enjoying tomorrow today—planning and anticipating tomorrow's joy
  - o Intentional acts of kindness—and expecting nothing in return
  - o Visualization and imagery—seeing it in the mind
  - o Meditation—raising the mind above the now
  - o Deep breathing—better oxygenation
  - o Progressive muscle relaxation—squeeze and release
  - o The relaxation response—a form of meditation with excellent research support
  - o Namaste—a no contact greeting with added meaning

THE FIGHT-OR-FLIGHT RESPONSE

Sudden threats to life generate the most dramatic stress responses. The immediate changes—increased heart rate, breathing, blood pressure, and muscle tension—result from the rush of adrenaline. The response is so named because the resolution is either stand your ground and fight or use the increased energy to take flight.

This is a survival response. What is detrimental to health is:

- o The response is triggered by events that don't dissipate readily, so the body is in a prolonged fight-or-flight state.
- o There is no quick fix for the effects of stress on the whole person.
- o The negative effects accumulate over time and chronically impair function on all levels.

THERE IS NO QUICK FIX FOR THE EFFECTS OF STRESS ON THE WHOLE PERSON.

******

SPIRITUAL STRESS

I see spiritual stress as events, information, and behaviors that tend to create doubts in deeply held beliefs and practices connected to the origin and purpose of life, the role of a higher power, and beliefs in the hereafter.

These doubts and questions can come from people.

o   When a friend or colleague, who used to share common beliefs asks: "How can you still hold on to these myths and anecdotes?" That is a source of spiritual challenge.
o   When reading literature or listening to an expert, they point out how wrong and delusional some of your most cherished beliefs are, in their opinion.
o   When you witness how evil humans can be in their treatment of one another. Our history bears witness to the inhumanity we can bring in oppressing people for material, territorial, or social gain.

All religions and philosophies have had critics, doubters, and unbelievers. As one of the physical and psychological stress outcomes is to make the individual more stress-resistant, spiritual stress may have a similar effect.

SPIRITUAL STRESS MANAGEMENT

Several analogies and practical skills come to mind:

o Review your beliefs. As new understanding and wisdom emerge, examine long-held beliefs to see if adjustments are needed.

o Find the principles in your belief system that generate experiences of spiritual rest, calm, cleansing, strength, comfort, forgiveness, redemption, hope, and daily help, especially in times of trouble.

To make this understanding practical in your life, I suggest you survey the protocols given in Appendix 1 and pick a few you can do easily or learn within a comfortable timeframe. Set up a plan to maintain these skills so they become a part of your life habits.

My experience and practice for triggering the relaxation response began in the classroom. (You may want to take a free or inexpensive class in learning stress reduction skills.) Teaching the skill and using it to meet a real need made it part of my automatic response. It has been so much a part of my reflex reaction that on one occasion, I felt concerned when a major threat occurred and my fight-or-flight reaction was not triggered.

HERE'S THAT STORY:

My wife and I were driving on the beltway between Washington, DC, and Northern Virginia. Traffic was heavy but moving at a good 50 mph. As we approached the American Legion Bridge, the car ahead of us blew a tire and swerved directly in front of us. I was able to maneuver around that car without getting in the way of the traffic on the right side. After that escape, I realized my fight-or-flight response did not trigger—no sudden increase in heart rate, no surge in blood pressure, no sense of fear for life.

I wondered aloud: could a person become stress-resistant to the point where life-threatening events do not trigger the programmed survival reaction? Is that good or bad?

****

As you review the physiology of stress, and techniques and skills to reduce and manage the stresses of life, what comments, questions, or stories come to mind?

NOTES FOR YOUR BOOK

10

WORK AND REST FOR BODY AND SOUL

'Tis better to have loved and lost,
than never to have loved at all.

—Alfred Lord Tennyson

I have combined these two subjects because they are so closely related, and I don't want to bore my readers with a lot of details. There is no need to make a case that exercise and rest are important to health, wellness, and happiness—that is well established. We shall accept that as a given, review the benefits, share ideas on what seems to work for different age groups, and give added encouragement to follow through on desirable goals.

WORK FOR THE BODY

The human body is built to do work and all organ systems are designed to perform special functions. The heart pumps, the lungs cycle air in and out, the brain constantly hums with processing tasks, and the skeletal and muscular systems generate force to produce movement.

Similar to the *Dietary Guidelines for Americans*, the US government health agencies have task forces that work on *Physical Activity Guidelines for Americans*. Since these guidelines are developed with a thorough review of international research in the field, the recommendations are applicable worldwide. The most recent guidelines were published in 2018.[1]

These guidelines are reviewed constantly with emphasis on what works, and how to get people using what works. The May 2020 revision of the Center for Disease Control (CDC) webpage on the health benefits of physical activity lists the following:[2]

o Immediate benefits include improved thinking, reduced short-term feelings of anxiety, sharpened learning, and judgment skills.

o It supports weight management because any amount of physical activity burns calories. Work your way up to 150 minutes a week of moderate activity to help control weight. To lose weight, incorporate a higher level of activity. There are calculators and calorie intake guidelines to help in planning.[3, 4]

o It reduces health risks including heart disease and stroke, two leading causes of death. Moderate to intense activity lowers blood pressure and cholesterol levels, reduces risks of diabetes and metabolic syndrome, and reduces risks of cancers of the bladder, breast, colon, endometrium, esophagus, kidney, lung, and stomach.

o It benefits the skeletal and muscular systems by slowing bone loss, reducing the risk of falling, helping relieve arthritis and rheumatism pain, and maintaining muscle strength.

o It improves the ability to do daily activities such as personal care, shopping, and meal preparation as you age.

o It increases the chances of living longer, with more healthy years. People who engage in moderate to vigorous activity for at least 150 minutes per week have a 33% lower risk of death from all causes when compared to predominantly inactive people.

THE KEY GUIDELINES ARE:

o Preschool aged children should be physically active most of their waking hours.
o Caregivers of preschool children should encourage active play with a variety of activity types.
o Children and adolescents should do 60 minutes or more of moderate to vigorous activity daily. Most of the 60 minutes should be aerobic, with muscle strengthening three times per week.
o Adults should keep in mind any amount of activity is better than sitting down or spending time in bed when not sleeping. The recommendation is two and a half to five hours of moderate to vigorous activity each week, but additional time yields more health benefits when done without risking damage to muscles and joints.
o Older adults should aim to stay within the adult recommendations, but keep vigorous effort to about 80% of maximum heart rate. They should add activities that help maintain balance, strengthen muscles, and adjust activities to accommodate functional limitations while challenging the limitations. They can also explore activities that allow for their best level of effort given the continual decline of abilities, or advancement of chronic health problems.
o Pregnant women can continue most exercise activities during pregnancy and post-partum. The healthcare provider can suggest adjustments if needed.

Choosing enjoyable activities is a huge part of keeping active. Not only does it make it more likely you'll stick with the activity, but the release of pleasure chemicals in the brain is an added benefit—dopamine, serotonin, and endorphins enhance mood, lessen pain, and generate a sense of reward for the effort.

If you have been inactive for a long period of time, these recommendations may help you get started:

o Start slowly and build up toward the goal of 150–300 minutes per week, and spread out the activities to allow time for recovery and healing.

o Choose activities you have enjoyed in the past or think you will enjoy.

o Understand the risks of the activity and take precautions to minimize them but approach any new activity with confidence.

o Prepare with appropriate gear, and make sure you follow rules, policies, and safety advice. For example, at 70 years of age, you may not want to celebrate a win in tennis by running up and jumping over the net like you did at 35. You might still be able to do it, but you're more likely to get hurt.

o Always check with your healthcare provider before changing your level of physical activity.

Information that promotes health serves no purpose unless it is used. So, the challenge is to get individuals, families, and communities reaching levels of physical activity that promote wellness and happiness.

Three key factors affect how we achieve the optimum level of work to gain the health benefits:

o Frequency—do some activity every day but moderate to high exertion every other day.

o Intensity—work at the recommended maximum heart rate for your age. Find an approximate rate by subtracting your age from 220. Then, multiply that number by 0.5 to get 50%, by 0.7 to get 70%, etc. Moderate exercise is 50–70 percent of maximum heart rate. Vigorous exercise is 70–85 percent.[5]

o Duration—although 30 minutes to an hour is a good gauge for an exercise session, research shows doing several ten-minute sessions throughout the day can give the same benefit.[6]

You may have heard of a 10,000-steps walking goal per day. While it is a reasonable goal, there is no research to support this specific number. That number came from the marketing campaign for one of the first pedometers introduced in Japan. The company gave the step tracker a Japanese name which, when translated to English, means "the 10,000-step meter."[7]

In the USA, there is help everywhere. In most counties and cities, Parks and Recreation Departments offer various programs to keep people active. From swimming and walking to sports leagues, there are choices to meet the needs of all ages and preferences. Nationally, the CDC and Department of Health and Human Services have publicized programs such as the "Move Your Way Campaign."[8]

Most countries offer similar programs for their citizens. Thanks to the internet, this information is available anywhere in the world. Still, the key is finding the motivation to act on the information, and the support to keep at it.

****

I have been very fortunate when it comes to physical activity because I am addicted to competition. Though the intensity of the activities has changed over the years, competition still motivates me.

When our kids were between six and sixteen, several families from the Southern Asian community got the fathers and all their children out to the soccer field every Sunday morning for two to three hours. Around that time in 1981, I discovered racquetball and played at least three times per week for 32 years.

When I retired, I switched from racquetball to pickleball. We have played at least three times per week since the spring of 2014. One of the hardest parts of the social isolation and distancing required in 2020 was having to give up pickleball.

I had a neatly packaged, fun routine three days each week—Monday, Wednesday, and Friday. Between 8:00 a.m. and 8:15 a.m., I arrived at the gym and did my stretching routine designed to involve every muscle and joint, for 10–15 minutes. (I picked the stretches from *Harvard Health's 35 Stretches*.[9] I chose the ones that would strengthen the lower back, and added yoga poses such as the cobra, bridge, crab, and child's pose.)

After stretching, I did 30 minutes of weight and resistance machines for muscle strengthening. Then, I'd get to the pickleball court between 9:00 a.m. and 9:15 a.m., play for two hours and get home around noon. How I miss this routine! What a beautiful way to celebrate retirement!

Then, social isolation and distancing put a halt to my routine. To find substitute activities, I started to walk for aerobic exercise and used dumbbells for strengthening. I found these to be poor substitutes for the joy and socializing of the gym and the pickleball court.

When addicted to an activity, you don't need outside motivation and encouragement. On pickleball days, I would wake up before my alarm went off. To keep motivation for my walking routine, I needed extra help. My two sons decided to establish a daily group chat so that we could share our goals and accomplishments.

When I felt like skipping my walk, I thought about not having anything to share on the chat at the end of the day. Posting a screenshot of my trail with the number of steps and miles walked, seemed to push me to get out and do it. (I used the Samsung Health App to track my walk.)

Getting your recommended minutes of activity each week is a major part of a wellness lifestyle. The benefits are real and scientifically verified.

****

WORK FOR THE SOUL

So, does the soul need exercise? If by *soul* we are talking about a person's deep sense of self and beliefs, then yes, there is work in the struggle to reconcile contradictions about life and the universe. Effort and energy are expended to examine and defend

> I HAD TO EXAMINE MY BELIEFS ABOUT THE NATURE AND EXISTENCE OF GOD.

cherished beliefs. I would suggest making an effort to understand how beliefs can change and expand with exposure to other viewpoints and other sources of data.

One of my struggles has been fitting my deep religious beliefs with my 12 years of training in the biological sciences. I had to examine my beliefs about the nature and existence of God.

My concepts ranged from childhood beliefs that God lived just above the blue of the sky. If you penetrate the blue, you'll be ushered into a great hallway leading to a huge throne on which a magnificent old man sits and commands every law and action in the universe. In my mind, God's main function was to oversee the work of angels who kept a detailed log—by longhand on scrolls of parchment—of everything I did and said, to determine if I should go to hell or heaven. This God was always a serious

God of justice and vengeance who would destroy by flood or fire, and who commanded people to destroy those who did not believe in Him.

Then in high school, I learned about space—beyond the blue. That placed God much farther removed from Earth.

Somewhere in my graduate education, as I punched my first data cards to enter information into the first mainframe computer on campus, I wondered if God had computers instead of the quills and scrolls I had imagined as a child. Then, holograms, laptops, hand-held computers with GPS, and Zoom became common and I wondered, what computer language does heaven use?

One of my most demanding pieces of spiritual work was to digest the 2006 book, *The G.O.D Experiments: How Science is Discovering God in Everything Including Us*, by Gary E. Schwartz, PhD, a psychologist at the University of Arizona. The gist of his argument was there could be laws of physics that operate to give guidance (G), organization (O) and design (D) in the universe, just as gravity and electromagnetism are laws we currently understand. Those laws would take the place of a *personal* God.

Another episode of soul-work was triggered in a biology laboratory by an incident I labelled "Me and My Paramecium." My assignment that day was to describe the physical features and behavior of a paramecium in a petri dish under a dissecting microscope. A paramecium is a single-cell organism with many short projections called cilia on its body. With these cilia, it swims from one side of the dish to the other, bumps into the dish, then heads off tail-first to the other side. That's all it did as far as I could tell.

So, there I am bending over the microscope, drawing in my notebook when these thoughts pop into my head: if, according to evolutionary theory, a single-cell organism is part of my ancestry, what a great distance exists between that active single-cell and the active observer. So, if evolution can create that distance, why would it stop at humans? Given billions of years, could life have evolved that could observe me like I was observing this creature in its dish? Am I somebody's paramecium?

This work of the soul, does it happen to everybody? I believe it does to some extent. The questions about our human existence and purpose naturally calls it out. The work, struggle, and search eventually find rest and satisfaction for those who find lasting happiness.

****

Rest for the Body

If work is the expenditure of energy, rest must be the cessation of work. Of course, complete cessation of work for the body is the total rest of death. So, the rest we will discuss here is sleep, relaxation, and leisure activities.

The Health Benefits of Sleep

The body cannot survive in a continuous awake state. Recent experiments with fruit flies, and on rats in the 1980s, show they die faster from sleep deprivation than from starvation.[10]

Sleep is necessary for all levels of function in the body. It is a basic need just as breath, food, and water are basic needs to support life. A summary of the benefits of regular sleep shows:[11]

o Better mental health: learning, decision-making, memory, problem-solving, creativity, coping skills, and emotional balance are improved, and less depression

o Better physical health: fewer infections, and lower risk of heart disease, kidney disease, strokes, obesity, and injury

o All systems and tissues positively affected: metabolic processes and effectiveness of insulin, hormone levels, tissue repair and healing, balance between hunger hormones (ghrelin and leptin) to regulate the appetite, and improved blood pressure regulation

The major overall function of sleep is to shutdown information inputs so the brain can process, catalog, sort, file, record, and store the information that it accumulated during waking hours. It needs to reset the baseline of chemicals and electrical circuitry in preparation for the next period of input.[12]

THE SLEEP CYCLE

Sleep fits into a 24-hour cycle, commonly called the circadian rhythm. Brain chemistry produces chemicals such as adenosine during waking hours, which slowly builds up and turns down brain function. This brings on sleepiness. (Caffeine is a competitor to adenosine and produces its anti-sleep effects by blocking adenosine from binding to brain cells.) As darkness comes on, the hormone melatonin increases and further reduces brain stem function to promote and sustain sleep.

The sleep cycle has two distinct phases: deep sleep—also called non-REM or slow wave sleep—and REM sleep, which refers to the rapid eye movement which occurs while dreaming. These two phases of sleep together last approximately 90 minutes, and we need four to five such cycles to get the full benefits of sleep. The need for several cycles varies, so some adults can get by on four cycles (six hours of sleep), while some need six (nine hours of sleep). Of course, there are also extremes at both ends, but on average, seven to eight hours fill the needs for most people.

It seems the healing, restorative functions, energy balancing, and immune system and hormone balancing take place during non-REM sleep. The brain shows increased activity during REM sleep and creates dreams as it fits new information into old files.

On awaking from sleep, growth hormone and cortisol are at their highest levels. This affects body tissues and energy balance in preparation for the day's activities.

We cannot completely recover sleep loss. Naps during the day help to make up for loss if taken at a time that does not impact the regular sleep cycle.

A recent study suggests short naps (15–20 minutes) during the workday help to increase worker productivity. Several companies are experimenting with "nap pods" for workers. However, the US Government has taken the position that sleep is prohibited in federal buildings.[13]

Recent surveys show up to 19 % of adults in the US report not getting enough sleep, and 50–70 million have chronic sleep disorders.[14] The two most common sleep disorders are sleep apnea (interrupted breathing during sleep), and insomnia (difficulty falling asleep and sustaining sleep). Correct diagnosis and medical assistance may be required for sleep apnea.

For insomnia, the first-level recommendations are to adjust sleep time and conditions in these ways:

o   Wind down with a period of quiet time before bed.
o   Ensure a darkened room.
o   Have a light evening meal with no alcohol, nicotine, or caffeine.
o   Reduce screen time before bed.
o   Maintain a regular sleep schedule even on weekends and holidays.

Rest for the body includes periodic relaxation during work hours and leisure activities to break the routine. Relaxation can be simply changing work positions, actively paying attention to the tension that exists in muscles and joints, and purposely relaxing those parts. (See Appendix 1 for relaxation and deep breathing techniques.)

If you can afford it, massage therapy has positive physical and mental benefits. Vacations and leisure activities outside of work, contribute to change and diversion for both body and mind.

****

REST FOR THE SOUL

If soul work is to wrestle, examine, adjust, and defend beliefs, what might rest for the soul look like? In this context, rest comes from resolution of doubt, acceptance that some things can't be proven, and shedding the responsibility to defend your beliefs. To come to that place is to find spiritual rest.

Whether we invoke faith or resignation that we cannot examine most spiritual matters with science, we reach a comfortable existence with what is functional in our philosophy and religious practices.

Spiritual rest can also apply to unloading guilt, worry, fears, insecurity, hopelessness, and concerns about world affairs (political unrest, climate threats, famines, other natural disasters, racial/gender issues etc) from the mind. Claiming inner peace in a troubled world is good rest. However, that claim is not effective as only an intellectual exercise. It must be a bedrock for living. If your religion or philosophy does not contribute inner peace to your life, then there is work to do—examine, search, and resolve. In other words, work to find rest.

As you review the benefits of exercise and rest to your health and happiness, what comments, questions, or stories come to mind?

NOTES FOR YOUR BOOK

11

GROWTH AND REPRODUCTION OF BODY AND SOUL

Love makes your soul crawl out from its hiding place.

—Zora Neale Hurston

I'll resist the temptation of giving a full lecture on human development and reproductive physiology. A very brief overview will suffice for purposes of connecting growth and reproduction to love, wellness, and happiness.

The summary presented here is a distillation of current information from reliable sources accessed on the Internet. I am using readily available sources so that, if you so choose, you can check it out for yourself in order to make practical, informed decisions.

You may have questions like when does a fertilized egg become a person? Or, can parents select the gender of their baby? I may not address each topic, but within the resources provided, you will find answers.

The highlights and terminology for development from a single cell at fertilization through birth are as follows:

o The production of gametes, ovum (egg), and spermatozoan (sperm) is different. A human female is born with all the eggs she will ever produce—about one to two million. These continuously die off so by puberty, there are only 400,000–600,000 remaining. During the average female reproductive years, only 400–500 will mature to produce fertilizable eggs. By menopause, zero eggs remain.[1]

o A male begins to produce sperm at puberty. Viable sperm production can continue well into age 70 and beyond.

o Fertilization—the fusion of a sperm and an egg forms a single-cell zygote.

o The zygote doubles its cells by a process called mitosis, and at the 16-cell stage is called a morula—a solid mass of cells. (If fertilization is in vitro, doctors can extract one cell for genetic examination at the four or eight-cell stage, including gender determination, without negative effects on further development.)

o The stages of development are as follows:
  o Germinal—fertilization to implantation
  o Embryonic—implantation to week 8
  o Fetal—week 9 to birth

o About four days after fertilization, the morula changes to a hollow mass of 32–256 cells called a blastocyst.

o At about the sixth to the eighth day after fertilization, the blastocyst attaches to the uterine wall—implantation.

o From implantation to the eighth week of growth, the developing offspring is called an embryo.

o Most organs form by week ten, with a rudimentary heart starting to beat at around week five.

o The last organs to form and develop are the brain and the nervous system.

○ Gestation is an average of 40 weeks, counting from the first day of the last menstrual period before pregnancy.

○ Approximately 50% of all fertilized eggs are lost before or shortly after implantation. Estimates are only 38% of fertilized eggs produce live births.

○ Birth hormones released by the fetus and placenta (cortisol and small amounts of oxytocin) trigger labor, which causes the release of a combination of hormones by the mother. For full-term vaginal delivery, the major actions are orchestrated by oxytocin and estrogens for uterine contraction, vasopressin for fluid balance, relaxin for joints and ligament relaxation, endorphins for pain reduction, and adrenaline and noradrenaline for blood pressure support.

DEVELOPMENTAL STAGES FOLLOWING BIRTH

This summary seeks to combine ideas from developmental psychologists such as Freud (psychosexual stages), Erik Erickson (eight life-span stages), Piaget (cognitive development), Kohlberg (moral development), and Ainsworth (attachment).[2]

Also, findings from recent studies on actual large-scale child neglect cases triggered by the Romanian Homes for Irrecoverable Children are included.[3]

Of course, the following stages and processes are in years and have much variability.

The physical, cognitive and psychosocial stages of growth have been studied and categorized as follows:

○ 0–2: The foundation is laid for feelings of love, security, attachment, trust, sensorimotor skills, vocalization, and start of language skills.

○ 2–4: There is rapid brain development called "blooming." (Although humans are born with all the brain cells they will have, interconnections and "brain circuitry" increase with stimulation and input. Childhood "blooming" is followed by "pruning," when neural connections are shaped into discreet circuits.) Developing abilities include physical dexterity, language, egocentric behavior, sharing, and autonomy.

o   4–6: Abilities that emerge at this stage include initiative versus guilt, language skills, behavior driven by avoiding punishment and by getting reward, physical dexterity, cognitive understanding that other people have beliefs, feelings, and thoughts that are different, and recognition of gender differences.

o   7–11: This stage lays down the patterns for industry versus inferiority, conventional morality, social approval driving behavior, understanding concrete events, time concepts, goals, language, and math skills.

o   12–18: Emerging qualities at this stage include identity versus confusion, abstract reasoning, logic and moral reasoning, identity formation with filtered feedback from the environment, marked effect of parenting style whether authoritative, authoritarian, permissive or uninvolved, independence and autonomy with physical and sexual maturity, foundation for intimacy, cognitive empathy, and balancing social order and individual rights.

o   19–29: Growth in young adulthood include intimacy versus isolation, marriage and family planning, solidifying moral principles, identity exploration, becoming self-supporting, and reaching the peak of physical abilities.

o   30–40: Early adulthood brings generativity versus stagnation, contribution to society, productivity, culture, waning of some physical abilities, cognitive abilities peak, moral behavior stabilizes, and parenting style settled.

o   40–64: Middle adulthood enables generativity, establishes legacy, work and social relationships, settles with religion and morality, shows physical decline, begins to decline cognitively, relinquishes parental roles, and surrenders the active role in the relationship with children.

o 65 and Over: This is a very evaluative phase of life involving integrity versus despair, satisfaction or regret, preparation for end of life as abilities decline physically, cognitively, and socially, and end-of-life pre-planning with medical directives.

****

GROWTH AND REPRODUCTION OF THE SOUL

A brief review of human development brings up questions about what else is there. Is the biology of life all there is to existence? I think not. That is why I combine thoughts about "growth and reproduction of the soul" with the physical, cognitive and psychological aspects.

THIS RETROSPECTIVE ON LIFE IS WHAT I REFER TO AS THE SPIRITUAL SIDE OF GROWTH AND REPRODUCTION.

I believe at some point in life, each human being, as long as the mind is functional and realistic, asks questions about the meaning of life, the origin of life on earth, and the measures of satisfaction having lived an average lifespan. These questions are most relevant if you have lived beyond 70 years. This retrospective on life is what I refer to as the spiritual side of growth and reproduction. This is the deep, inner sense of evaluation, review, and harmonizing events with beliefs, hopes, and dreams.

For parts of the story that is beyond memory, parents and other relatives should pass on to a child the story surrounding their beginning and early life. Of course, it is easier to pass on pleasant, exciting stories. For the unpleasant, traumatic, or dark stories, it is better to gauge psychological readiness, if possible.

My best approach to what I mean by "Growth and Reproduction of the Soul" is to share my life retrospective by stages.

SENSE OF SELF AND DESTINY SET IN CHILDHOOD—CHANGES OVER THE LIFESPAN

I was born fifth in a family of eleven children. From my memories, and what parents and siblings shared, I see the following details having major influences on how my life unfolded.

- o My parents experienced a really rough segment of their life when their fourth child died from pneumonia at two years of age. They were in the process of joining the Seventh-Day Adventist church, and my mother was pregnant with me when they got baptized.
- o I was a hot-tempered, cross-eyed, left-handed child in a minority Indian community, and got teased on all four accounts. At the time, schoolteachers believed left-handers should be changed to right-handedness. The mode of conversion was for the teacher to strike you with a wooden ruler on the left-hand while you did your penmanship! My buddy, Leroy Morgan, worked out a strategy to get me around those knuckle assaults. He did his penmanship work, gave me his paper on which I pretended to write with my right hand, then did my work in a disguise of his handwriting. We switched papers back when the teacher was not looking. I never converted.
- o Sexual identity and awareness arrived at five years of age. I still have vivid memories of the process, the personalities, and the encounters that shaped my sexual orientation and laid the foundation for an exciting life as a husband. (I think a mixture of Freud's psychosexual stage, Erickson's psychosocial stage, and Piaget's cognitive development were clearly visible in my experiences.)

o I started in school as a slow learner with extreme self-consciousness (most likely related to being cross-eyed and left-handed). After reaching Standard One (British system, equivalent to Grade 2 in the American system), and getting a new teacher, things clicked into place. It seems that my learning/memorizing circuits blossomed, and throughout elementary and high school, I was top of the class.

o I loved vigorous play and ran at full speed in the game of catch we called "coop." During afternoon recess one day, I jumped over an embankment, slid on some loose gravel, and broke my left leg at mid-thigh. There was no phone or vehicle in the village, so four of the older boys had to carry me on a stretcher, along an unpaved road to the clinic one mile away. That day, I saw my mother cry in public for the first time as she saw me lifted onto the stretcher. I was ten years old and spent three months in the hospital in traction.

o Between 7 and 12 years old, my concept of the end of the world, shortness of time, and life after this life became very defined, and I looked at the future within those concepts. The world was supposed to end in five years, according to all the sermons and worship talks from our elders and pastors. When baptized by immersion in the river at 11, I distinctly remember feeling so holy that I was ready to fly through the sky and walk the streets of gold. I took church and religion very seriously, always with a sense of never being good enough no matter how hard I tried to keep all the rules.

o My high school years began at 13 years old. I started out walking from our village to the schoolhouse on the hill at a place called Perseverance, about two miles from home. I continued to excel in schoolwork. An older relative in the village seemed to have singled me out for the name "Madras Coolie." I finished high school as the only graduate in the class when others dropped out or did not qualify for the Cambridge Exams. (Cambridge University in England administered graduating exams to all high schools in the British colonies at the time.)

o At 17.5 years of age, I had the epiphany of the strong conviction that I was destined to be a traveling evangelist among the Caribbean islands. I performed in a play on the life of St. Paul, the apostle, in which I had to memorize and deliver all of Paul's major speeches. Also, convinced that I would have a son as my first child, I settled on his name, Michael Fitzgerald. (He is 48 years old as I write this.)

o At 18, I started to teach in the high school from which I graduated and became principal for one year at 19. As a lay preacher on the church's regular schedule, my greatest enjoyment was preparing and delivering sermons. At the time, I felt if I preached loudly enough, long enough, and frequently enough, I could hasten the coming of Christ and the end of the world! I left for college in the USA at 21.

o At Andrews University in Berrien Springs, MI, I gave in to my mother's wishes and enrolled as a pre-med major instead of following my conviction to do theology.

o The highlights of my adjustments to changing circumstances during that period included:

    o Switching college majors from pre-med to medical technology

    o Fighting the mental and social battles of fostering an inter-racial relationship in the late 1960s

    o Experimenting with "the Shettles technique" to see if my wife and I could tip the odds in favor of having a boy as our first child[4]

- o Working full-time while taking graduate programs in biology at Andrews University and Michigan State University
  - o Serving a three-year postdoctoral research fellowship at the University of Virginia.
- o Events unfolded in quick succession that led to quitting college teaching, filing bankruptcy, changing fields of professional interest, and designing two college courses in health and wellness.
- o By 40 years of age, I had a full-time job with the heart surgery team at Washington Hospital Center. Our children were then 14, 12, and 9, and my wife worked outside the home because a one-salary household couldn't make it as a lower-middle-class family.
- o In all of this, I still believed the end of the world would take place around the year 2000. That belief influenced my preparation for retirement. It wasn't until about 2005 when I was back in college teaching that I mentally came to terms with the idea I would one day retire, grow old, and die. As the sponsor for a group of students attending the General Youth Conference, I met with the group each evening to hear reactions to the day's presentations. One was very troubled with the theme of the sermon she had just heard that day. The entire presentation was about why the world would end in about three years. Just accepted into medical school, her question was, "If these things are really true, why should I bother to go to medical school?" I shared my once-held convictions about the year 2000. That helped her settle the question. I imagine she now has a thriving medical practice 15 years later.
- o Comfortable in retirement now, I look forward to my 75th birthday in 2021. With two granddaughters and two grandsons, I think I will live to see a great-grandchild. I am comfortable preparing for end-of-life issues. My wife

has reached that point of comfort and acceptance that our time is very limited. We have chosen cremation as our exit strategy, and hospice care at home before that day comes. And we project our next few years in the peace that we have had a good life. We are no longer waiting for translation and freely discuss our preferences—she wants to go first, in her sleep. I want to go during a nap after an early game of pickleball and hot sex, followed by the final sleep. (I keep my Cialis prescription on continuous refill, and my wife said she'll leave instructions for an arrangement!)

The spiritual side of growth and reproduction for us is making sense of how life has transpired, accepting the frailties of our humanity, facing our mortality with peace, finding meaning in having lived by some basic convictions about the goodness of human beings, seeing our children become happy adults, enjoying our grandchildren, and enjoying the life that is, while anticipating some simple joys in the few years left.

I hope you find a comfortable sense of love, wellness, and happiness as you review your life.

Notes for Your Book

_____

_____

_____

_____

_____

_____

_____

_____

_____

_____

_____

_____

_____

_____

_____

_____

_____

_____

_____

_____

_____

_____

_____

_____

_____

_____

_____

PART 3

YOUR BEST WARRIOR, MIRACLE-WORKER, LOVER, AND RULER

Wid a betta katta, you can joge
a bigga stone.

—A Vincy Proverb by Uncle Vertyl

(Translation: With a better pad for you head, you can carry a larger stone. "Vincy" is a colloquialism for someone from St. Vincent & the Grenadines.)

12

YOUR INNER WARRIOR, MIRACLE-WORKER, LOVER, AND RULER

It takes courage to love, but pain through love is the
purifying fire which those who love generously know.

—Eleanor Roosevelt

Carl Jung's concepts have contributed a lot to the synthesis I achieved in organizing my teaching framework. The archetypes (symbols that embody a set of qualities) attracted my attention as I helped lead coaching sessions at major employers in the Washington, DC area. Our coach team leader was Master Coach, Joan Wangler, who is now a senior coach with the Center for Excellence in Public Leadership at George Washington University.[1]

One coaching session was anchored on the research and applications published by Robert Moore and Douglas Gillette in their 1990 book titled, *King, Warrior, Magician, Lover: Rediscovering the Archetypes of the Mature Male.*[2] I connected that concept to my four loves foundation, and to the qualities of Christ, the essence of Christianity. I changed "Magician" to "Miracle-Worker" to fit better with my Christian beliefs, and "King" to "Ruler," to make it applicable to all positions of leadership, genders, and age groups.

Each archetype has an immature form along with a negative and positive side. My useable extract from the research and case examples was to identify and encourage growth in the positive side. Here's a list of the positive qualities associated with each archetype:

- o **The Warrior**
  adaptable, alert, assertive, can-do attitude, clarity of mission, committed, constructively aggressive, courageous, decisive, disciplined, enduring, energetic, fearless, fighting good fights, flexible, loyal, mentally tough, persevering, realistic, reflexive, self-confident, self-controlled, self-denying, skillful, strategic, strong, tactician, trained.

- o **The Miracle-Worker**
  amazing, bold, clearsighted, confident, discerning, extraordinary, healing, initiator, insightful, intuitive, meditative, perceptive, powerful of mind, self-aware, self-reflective, synthesizing, technical, thoughtful, timeless, transformative, transcendental thinkers, unconfined, visionary, wise.

- o **The Lover**
  anchored, compassionate, connected, creative, deliberate, emotional, empathetic, enduring, energizing, enthusiastic, ethical, forgiving, generous, gentle, hopeful, humble, imaginative, inspirational, joyful, kind, moral, mysterious, optimistic, passionate, patient, romantic, sacrificial, sensitive, sensual, sentimental, spiritual, spontaneous, tender, unifying, zestful.

o **The Ruler**

affirming, benevolent, blessed, calmly reassuring, cheerful, clarity of purpose, commanding, compassionate, congratulatory, contagiously optimistic, courageous, decisive, devoted, elegant, empathetic, encouraging, fertile, flourishing, friendly, fruitful, generates stability, generative, honest, hopeful, inspirational, integrative, just, leader by example, loyal, magnanimous, merciful, nurturing, offers recognition, organized, peace loving, peace seeking, pleasantly authoritative, promoting, providing for prosperity, prudent, rational, realistic greatness, reasonable, redemptive, responsible, savior, self-discipline, servant leader, stewardship, temperate, tolerant, wise.

From the perspective that the Christ of Christianity is the perfect example of all these positive qualities, I added the idea of growth to maturity in Christ as the ultimate goal for living at our best. This addition to the original framework resulted in this matrix:

Maturity in C H R I S T

WARRIOR	MIRACLE WORKER	LOVER	KING RULER
STRENGTH	MIND	HEART	SOUL
PHYSIOLOGIC	MENTAL	PSYCHO SOCIAL	SPIRITUAL
EROS	STORGE	PHILIA	AGAPE

LOVE is the foundation. The second row is whole-person function. The third row is the dimensions in which Christ said humans should love God—with heart, soul, mind, and strength (Mark 12:30). The top row is the embodiment of all positive qualities as exhibited in the life of Christ.

With this outline, I proposed a college-level course titled "Christ-Centered Wellness." The emphasis in this course was that the practical goal of Christianity is growing to maturity in Christ. That is the highest level of wellness for a Christian. To get there, you can't just have a set of rules to regulate behavior. You have to put love in action, have the mind of Christ develop in you, and let that direct how you treat your fellow humans.

The course became a required course in the Health Management curriculum at Washington Adventist University from 2004 through 2018.

Along with the framework above, I had captured a few thoughts on love and wellness through my meditations on passages in the New Testament. For example, from the letter we know as Third John, I saw expressions of love and concern for health and prosperity from a mentor to fellow evangelist. I imagined the younger man's response was to see "wellness of the soul" was more important than "wellness of the body." Then, the principles of wellness of the soul, the easier state to attain, could be used to lend motivation and inspiration to the process of working for wellness of the body.

These ideas were captured in an article, "The Gaius Principle," published in the *Adventist Review*, the Seventh-day Adventist Church's worldwide magazine.[3] The key point here was "wellness of the soul" is more important than "wellness of the body." Since wellness of the soul is easier to attain, the principles involved may help to promote wellness of the body.

Similar meditative re-reading of the story of Christ's early disciples as recorded in Acts chapter two, while reading Malcolm Gladwell's book, *The Tipping Point*, led to ideas about the contagiousness of a message.[4] Gladwell said if a message were "sticky," if a few of the right people connect to that message, and if the context is right, sudden outbreaks of positive epidemics can happen.

I captured some applications to "Christ-centered Wellness" in an article titled "Let's Start a Wellness Epidemic."[5] If the core of Christianity—Christ's life, death, and resurrection—is the "sticky message," can the right people in the right context ignite "a Christ-centered wellness epidemic?"

As I adapted this framework, which matured in a course at a secular university over 15 years, to a Christian institution, it was a pleasure to see the scriptural connections and analogies in physiologic principles. I took the seven dynamic processes (homeostasis, nutrition, stress adaptation, work, rest, growth, and reproduction) in the framework and made ten applications. Homeostasis yielded four principles.

These principles are explained in more detail in the third article published in *Adventist Review* with the title "10 Health Principles for Body and Soul."[6] They are the physical and spiritual applications from water, DNA, energy, oxygen, nutrition, stress adaptation, work, rest, growth, and reproduction.

****

Another rest stop on the journey of fully developing the Christ-Centered Wellness course was winning a worldwide sermon competition. The Health Ministries department of the Seventh-day Adventist Church had developed a new educational model for teaching health principles. The key piece of this program was the acronym "CELEBRATIONS." Each letter in this acronym was the beginning of a word that captured a key concept of health: C for Choice, E for Exercise, L for Liquids, etc.

Before launching the CELEBRATIONS program, they announced a sermon competition for pastors and lay-preachers around the world. The winning sermon would be awarded $500-US, and the sermon would be published in the church's magazine, *Ministry*. My entry, "C is for What Matters Most," was declared the winner by judges in a blind contest.

However, the leaders of the Health Ministries department objected to the publication. Later on, I deduced since they had already committed to "C is for Choice," the winning sermon, which argued for "C is for Christ" would not support their concept. (The text of "C is for What Matters Most" is presented in Appendix 3.)

One of the many enjoyable parts of my story is how I got the opportunity to write the three articles for the *Adventist Review*. An assistant editor at the magazine, who was a former student in my "Healthier Living" class, called one day to ask if I would be interested in submitting an article "about some of the things we discussed in class." I had used the book *Personal Wellness: How to Go the Distance* as the textbook, and the class had done the exercise of constructing a notebook "as if you are writing a book." I was delighted to write and experience her editorial process. She was the one to bring the *Ministry* sermon competition to my attention.

****

The Christ-Centered Wellness course filled a 15-week semester. This allowed ample time for preliminary discussions of wellness, life purpose, mission and vision, happiness, and life fulfillment. We blocked out seven of the fifteen weeks for an exploration of what the disciples of Christ may have said and done during the 49 days between Christ's resurrection and the "Day of Pentecost." That 50th day after Christ's resurrection was when they became "filled with the Holy Spirit" (Acts 2:1–4) and changed the world.

Students prepared prior to class using a workbook, and the 1.3-hour class-time was devoted to open discussions. A variety of small groups and large group sharing was effective for this goal.

The educational strategy was to provide resources that led students to self-study and exploration. Then, they brought questions and summary ideas to share in the discussions.

The outline of the course is summarized as follows:

- **Week 1**
  - Your story—religious background, the current role religion plays in your life, life purpose, career goals, and mission. (This had an additional level of interest during discussions in the 2012–2018 school years as several students from Saudi Arabia took the course.)
  - The Christ-Centered Wellness framework—reading the three *Adventist Review* articles and writing a summary paper as the basis for group discussion
- **Week 2**
  - Reading the Gospel of John for a review the life of Christ, and 1st, 2nd, and 3rd John for practical ideas on love as the foundation of life for a Christian
  - Discussion of "The Gaius Principle;" and "Let's Start a Wellness Epidemic."
- **Week 3**
  - "10 Health Principles for Body and Soul"
  - Positive qualities of the Warrior, Miracle-Worker, Lover, and Ruler
- **Week 4**
  - Christ in your life—your story
  - Journaling and sharing
- **Week 5**
  - Preparation for the 7-week experiment and discussion of Acts 2.
  - Commitment to daily journaling, responding to the daily Scripture searches, writing your imagined conversations among the disciples, composing your "Dear God" prayers.

o **Weeks 6–12**
  o Day 1—imagine the start of the 49 days before the Day of Pentecost, review the events of resurrection Sunday, discuss the emotions and thoughts of the disciples compared with crucifixion Friday, resting on the Sabbath, the "Dear God" prayer, and journaling.
  o Day 2—reflect on crucifixion and resurrection and applications to your life—what needs crucifying and what needs resurrecting, "Dear God" prayer, and journaling.
  o Day 3—the disciples' doubts, disappointments and fears, *our* doubts, disappointments, and fears. Did Christ meet with them daily? What is our daily encounter with Christ? "Dear God," and journaling.
  o Day 4—the transformation: compare what you see of the disciples' personality and emotional state at this point (six days after Christ's crucifixion) with what they became after the 49 days of preparation; "Dear God," and journaling.
  o Day 5—imagine Christ leading an all-day seminar for the disciples. What might have been the topics of discussion? "Dear God" and journaling.
  o Day 6—discovery of how the disciples' experiences and ours may have parallels: transforming experiences; growth and changes in our beliefs; "Dear God," and journaling.
  o Day 7—the disciples are growing in their understanding, what might they have learned about love? What disclosures and confessions might they have made to one another? Our openness to disclosures and confessions, "Dear God," and journaling.
  o The personal exploration activities continued to Day 50 with the events of the Day of Pentecost. Everyone had time to share how the exploration affected their

lives, what scriptural passages applied, what practical decisions they made about their lives, and how their understanding and practical applications of love may have grown.

- o **Weeks 13–15**
  - o The final three weeks of the course were devoted to personal presentations to the large group about the impact of the exploration, reflecting on health of the body and soul, prosperity, and how to grow to maturity in Christ.
  - o Sharing impactful passages of Scripture such as: "Let this mind be in you which was also in Christ Jesus…" "For me to live is Christ…" "Christ in you, the hope…" "Be transformed by the renewing of your mind…"
  - o (We applied the analogy that, to followers of Christ, Scripture is the GPS on this road of life. It is more inspirational when individuals search for themselves instead of receiving the references to look up. In the search process, they may discover other passages, thoughts, or associations that may not be stirred if the selections were already made.)
  - o How to live like Jesus: blending Scripture, psychology, career plans, financial security, and impacting society through love for all.

This brief overview of a college level course titled "Christ-Centered Wellness" is presented to show how Christians may use the principles of "wellness of the soul" to promote "wellness of the body" and "wellness of society."

I had the opportunity to describe this course and its potential for research at Christian churches to Drs. Harold Koenig and Redford Williams at the *Center for Spirituality, Theology and Health* at Duke University Medical Center.[7]

They had me prepare a project outline and data collection protocol. They agreed that this could be done by randomizing participants into two groups. The seven-week process would be the treatment for the test group, and the usual lifestyle or any other health promotion process the control for those not assigned to the treatment group.

> I BELIEVE FOCUSING ON GROWTH TO MATURITY IN CHRIST CAN SOLVE A LOT OF INDIVIDUAL AND SOCIETAL PROBLEMS.

Research and good data collection take a lot of time and require funding. I was about to retire so I did not pursue the project. I hope one of my former students—or anyone who might be so inspired—could take it up as a future research project. In the meantime, I will present the ideas through this book, and in an online course conducted via Zoom.

I believe focusing on growth to maturity in Christ can solve a lot of individual and societal problems. Review the list of positive qualities, knowing that every individual is a unique blend of the Warrior, the Miracle-worker, the Lover, and the Ruler.

HERE'S MY PROPOSAL TO SOLVING PERSONAL AND WORLD PROBLEMS:

- o Examine yourself: look at the list of qualities above and see what in your life you should strengthen before you tell others what to do, before you try to change other people, and before you try to change the world. The psychological literature offers the idea that the Ruler archetype is the main energy source for living positive qualities. The qualities of the Lover, Miracle-Worker, and Warrior are energized by the Ruler. Each of us is a unique combination of the qualities of the four. A passage of Scripture that comes to mind is 1 Peter 2:9, "But you are a chosen people, a royal priesthood, a holy nation, God's special possession, that you may declare the praises of him who called you out of darkness into his wonderful light." I believe this holds for every individual Christian, not any one denomination of Christianity.

o Review how to *really* love others by following Christ's example. If you have Christian beliefs, then review the life of Christ as told in the Gospel of John, meditate on the advice given in 1st, 2nd, and 3rd John. If you are not Christian or don't tolerate Christian beliefs, review the philosophical/psychological writings that help shape your thinking. Review how to treat other humans with value, dignity, life-promoting help instead of destructive, punishing, even death-dealing approaches. (We have evolved way beyond settling differences as we did in the Crusades, civil wars, and world wars.)

o Re-read and study the stories of successful, non-violent protests to create social change. The lives of Mahatma Gandhi, Martin Luther King, Jr., Nelson Mandela, and Congressman John Lewis were not perfect, but great examples of non-violent revolutionaries.

The process of self-examination is both spiritual and psychological. Contemplate the summary in the diagram below. Whatever your belief system, self-examination leads to greater self-understanding, which generates higher self-acceptance and triggers learning self-management techniques, which results in higher self-actualization—satisfaction with life. A Christian focuses all these processes on growing to maturity in Christ.

Personal Responsibility for Wellness

Self-Examination
Self-Understanding

Self-Actualization

Personal Growth

Self-Acceptance

Self-Management

In wellness promotion, I have taken the stance to emphasize positive qualities and positive actions. This does not mean I overlook the negatives of human nature; each positive has an opposite. My teaching and coaching approach is: it is better psychology to be positive and let growth in the positives transform the negatives.

If someone wants to examine negative qualities, I recommend the recent research on "The Light Triad vs The Dark Triad of Personality" by Scott Barry Kaufman.[8] He identified three foundational qualities of the Light Triad: Humanism—valuing the dignity and worth of each individual; Kantianism—treating people as ends unto themselves and not mere means; Faith in Humanity—believing in the fundamental goodness of humanity.

The three foundational qualities of the Dark Triad are: Narcissism—self-importance; Machiavellianism—strategic exploitation and deceit; and Psychopathy—callousness and cynicism. Kaufman offers a free evaluation of Light Triad versus Dark Triad, as well as Self-Actualization Tests on his website.[9]

****

Again, I submit that most humans want to love and be loved, enjoy a long and healthy life, and sum it all up as a happy life. It seems to me that individuals strive to find their own way. Many individuals miss out and "live lives of quiet desperation, and die with their song still in them," as Thoreau famously said in Walden.[10]

Let's imagine life as a road-trip. How do we get to a destination? It is a combination of planning (with or without GPS), responding to changing circumstances as they arise (accidents, detours, stopping just to explore, or to go to the bathroom), and keeping on driving.

Two memorable road trips come to mind: one when I fell asleep at the wheel, and the other in a Chevy station-wagon with three kids at ages five years, three years, and eight months.

When our first son was one month old, we decided to drive from Berrien Springs, Michigan, to Toronto, Canada. We wanted to have his dedication ceremony performed by my eldest brother, Rick, the pastor of a large Christian church in downtown Toronto.

To get the most out of the drive, we decided to take the long route via the Upper Peninsula of Michigan. Instead of a seven-hour drive, we opted for the 11-hour route! It was such a relaxing trip I fell asleep while driving!

Fortunately, the shoulder of the road was wide enough and rough enough to wake me up just before I lost control of the car.

(You are never so wide awake as when you get shaken awake while driving!)

As I pulled back onto the pavement, I reached back into the car-bed on the floor of the backseat to touch our son. He was sleeping peacefully. My wife was startled but not panicked—she had dozed off too.

On the road of life, sometimes we fall asleep. When life events or world conditions shake us awake, they can catapult us into transforming action.

In this section of the book, I will outline a possible course of wide-awake action I believe can make a difference for individuals, whole communities, our nation, and the world.

****

The second road-trip, which is a fond memory for the whole family (except our baby-girl who was only eight months old at the time), was from East Lansing, Michigan, to Hollywood Beach, Florida. This was an exciting trip for several reasons.

I was making my first presentation of original research at an international scientific meeting. The university paid all our travel expenses. Our Chevrolet Caprice station-wagon, which the kids had named "Big Red," was in prime condition. Our five and three-year-old boys and eight-month-old daughter were good travelers.

My wife had spent time outfitting Big Red with a six-inch thick foam pad that filled the entire back end when we folded down the seats. That was our snoozing area at rest stops and the kids' play area while we drove. This was before seat-belt laws.

One of my top memories of that trip was we did not hear many queries of "Are we there yet?" We had looked ahead at fun places to stop and planned leisurely visits to enjoy the entertainment and food. Two such places were "South-of-the-Border," in South Carolina, and "Lion Country Safari" in Florida. This 2800-miles round trip created wonderful, pleasant memories captured on 35mm slides.

****

One of the ways to make the road-trip of life more satisfying is to help one another along the way. Current world conditions call for collaboration and provide opportunities to coordinate for the greater good.

Let's look at four very prominent challenges we faced in 2020. *(In the pages to follow, I will use the designation "PN-20" to represent all the conditions that resulted from the spread of the viral disease that shutdown the world economy, over-burdened healthcare systems, and caused over 2.5 million deaths. The virus and all its mutating variants will be designated "CV-19.")*

o PN-20 is still raging in the USA as I write this in February, 2021. Coordination and collaboration would go a long way in getting the general public to adhere to the practices of wearing masks in public, social distancing, and social isolation as needed. I believe one of the main reasons for the prolonged surge of the first wave of infections in the USA was lack of coordination and collaboration with public health experts. For this to happen, leaders must know their expertise and strengths, put aside political goals, and let the main goal be to subdue the infection.[11]

o There are major changes in the world economy as a consequence of PN-20. Job losses and the resulting reduction in productivity have created unexpected hardships, insecurities, and worry on personal and corporate levels.[12]

o There was a strong upswing in confronting race relations as a result of the death of George Floyd.[13] The details are mind-numbing when you watch the video and consider the range of human emotions involved on the part of the dying man, the police, the onlookers, the one who captured the video, and the protest marchers. This has triggered a review of several racially charged deadly confrontation cases with the police, calls for defunding police departments, and evaluation of other racist symbols as carried in the names of sports teams and memorials to the American Civil War. The Black Lives Matter movement is reminiscent of the civil rights fight of the

1950s and 1960s. (I'm writing this on July 17, 2020, the day Congressman John Lewis, the last of the "Big Six" leaders of the Civil Rights Movement died.)[14]

o   The workplace anti-discrimination ruling by the US Supreme Court has elevated the rights and status of LGBTQ+ citizens.[15, 16]

I highlight the above societal challenges as major issues currently needing solutions. Granted, many other societal and ecological problems face humanity, such as climate change, equal pay for women, homelessness, starvation, pollution, dwindling resources, and species extinction. I cannot deal with all of them in this focus on love, wellness, and happiness. It seems that 2020 focused attention on four problems that challenge how we regard and interact with one another.

My advice to students over my teaching career has been, "See a problem? Propose a solution." So, I would like to propose what I believe to be a comprehensive solution to the four problems above. My *road-trip* in life has taken me along a path that presented the experiences and knowledge to synthesize an approach for personal growth that examines the root of all the societal problems we face. Here is why I believe I am qualified to propose such a solution:

o   Through my struggles with the larger questions of life, I explored solutions within religious and secular fellowships. Using the growth/reproduction analogy, I see spirituality as a process of maturing according to your beliefs and assumptions. As you move from babyhood to a mature, reflective adulthood, your assumptions change. I hold on to the Christian principles that anchored my life and have shed some of the restrictive beliefs which made me feel superior to others. My growth has allowed me to separate "religion" from "spirituality." I anchor my solution on spirituality based on the essence of Christianity.

o   I have read and studied deeply into the theories of personality, behavior control, and positive psychology.

Let's get back to our examples of the four problems mentioned earlier.

o   **PN-20**
  o   In a list published in October 2019 of countries who had the resources, scientific expertise, finances, and facilities to cope with an outbreak like PN-20, the USA was rated as # 1.[17]
  o   The actual experience at six months of PN-20 showed that the USA, India and Brazil were leading the world in number of confirmed cases and confirmed deaths.[18] With only four percent of the world's population, the USA had 20 percent of the world's deaths from CV-19.
  o   Lessons learned: we have to subjugate personality and political differences for the cooperation it takes to handle large scale threats to life and health— the common good. Let scientific experts lead, and evaluate impulsive, off-the-cuff ideas before they are publicized. The lessons from this experience should set a very high level of preparedness for the next one. It was exciting to see a vaccine being produced in record time, and to receive the first shot of the Pfizer version on March 4, 2021, and the second shot three weeks later.

o   **The Economy**
  o   Some employees benefitted financially, socially, and physically from the office shutdowns and work at home policies. The suffering from job loss among

workers who can't do what they do from home created immediate hardships and future insecurities.[19]

o Government financial assistance helped to some degree. The community-level response was even more heart-warming. People reached out to one another with food and supplies. Churches and charitable organizations stepped up to respond to unexpected needs. Young people and children raised funds, distributed food, and reached out to strangers. A chord of genuine response to needs was struck. I believe it will remain vibrating and produce a long-lasting sense of community, better prepared for future disasters.

o **The racial divide**

o Race relations are deeply spiritual topics anchored in our deepest beliefs about the origin of humanity. How did it become ingrained in every culture that the darker skin colors are less desirable? How did paleness—resulting from lower melanin content—become more valued?

I believe five things influenced my attitudes, which I had to strive to rectify. I suggest that each of us needs to complete the self-examination and adjust where indicated.

- As children in a Christian church, we used to sing, "Satan makes my heart all black with sin. Jesus makes it white when he comes in. Whiter than the snow yes whiter than the snow. And when Satan tempts me, I'll say no, no, no!"
- In grade school, we had a textbook that explained all the various races on earth were descendants of Noah's three sons. Shem fathered the white races, Japheth

fathered the brown races, and Ham, fathered the black races. Then, there was a curse on Ham because he laughed at his father's nakedness, and the curse led to the enslavement of the black races.

· As a teenager, I heard one of the black women in the village shout out to a guy who was probably the deepest black in complexion of anyone I had seen: "Good for you, man, you raised your color!" He had just married the whitest girl in the village.

· I recall being in Manilla, Philippines, in the 1990s when there was a rash of poisoning due to people rubbing their skin with a mercury compound in hopes of lightening the skin color.

· Most slave traders and slave owners in the Americas and the Caribbean called themselves Christians.

THE LGBTQ+ COMMUNITY

After many years of suppression, discrimination, and marginalization, this group of citizens has achieved acceptance in many sectors. It seems acceptance within religious communities is still a struggle, but is getting better. For me, three ideas have contributed to my growth in attitudes toward members of this community:

o They are included in the command to love my neighbor.

o A secular state should not establish laws based on religious definitions of morality.

o The wording of the US Supreme Court ruling legalizing same-sex marriage is worth noting: "No union is more profound than marriage, for it embodies the highest ideals of love, fidelity, devotion, sacrifice, and family. In forming a marital union, two people become something greater than once they were. As some of the petitioners in these cases demonstrate, marriage embodies a love that may endure even past death. It would misunderstand these men and women to say they disrespect the idea of marriage. Their plea is that they do respect it, respect it so deeply that they seek to find its fulfillment for themselves. Their hope is not to be condemned to live in loneliness, excluded from one of civilization's oldest institutions. They ask for equal dignity in the eyes of the law. The Constitution grants them that right."[16]

> LOVE DOES NOT FORCE OTHERS TO BELIEVE WHAT WE BELIEVE.

Our beliefs about human origin and our concept of God and love affect how we treat people. Love does not force others to believe what we believe.

So, I've identified a few problems on the road of life, offered a solution as my knowledge, understanding, and experience allow me to, and plan to promote that solution. A summary of the solution is:

o Seek to understand love more fully, and make it practical in dealing with all human beings.
o Find examples of those who have tried to live up to the ideals of the positive qualities of which we are capable.
o For Christians, the perfect example is Christ.
o To grow to maturity in Christ through understanding love and treating all humans as equal in love is the path to a fulfilled life and happiness.
o The philosophical platform for action is captured in Galatians 3: 27, 28. *"For as many of you as were baptized into Christ, have put on Christ. There is neither Jew nor Greek, there is neither slave nor free, there is neither male nor female, for you are all one in Christ."*

Growing to maturity in Christ is the path to solving many divisions and problems in this world.

****

After I had constructed the course in Christ-Centered Wellness, I had a chance to share the concepts with Dr. Ben Carson in his office at Johns Hopkins University Medical Center. A mutual friend, who was dying of liver cancer, had introduced me to Dr. Carson.

He connected with the concepts and video-taped a message for us to use in our presentations. Then he gave us the following as the Foreword for the workbook we developed for the course:

> I like the concept of a wellness epidemic that is Christ-centered. Jesus Christ spent a considerable amount of time healing the sick. In fact, whenever he entered a new location, this seemed to be the initial priority. This gives us some insight into the divine importance placed on total health.
>
> In my work as a neurosurgeon, I have to deal with life and death situations frequently. I count it a great privilege to have been given a special talent and gift by God to intervene in people's lives and hopefully restore the most important thing that they have, their health.
>
> I can remember when I came to Johns Hopkins as an intern, I was very impressed with the kinds of patients that I found on the wards. There were CEOs of major corporations, heads of state, and members of royal families. In many cases, they were dying of malignant diseases. Every one of them would have given every penny and every title for a clean bill of health. It is said that most people do not consider how important their health is until they find themselves on their death bed.

It is very important that we cherish the gift of health and do everything that we can to maintain it. I am fond of saying that if everybody ate three well-balanced meals a day, drank six to eight glasses of pure water, got regular exercise and rest, did not put harmful substances into their bodies and made a conscious effort to reduce stress in their lives, most of us in the medical field would be looking for new jobs.

Reading this book and using some of its exercises is likely to be extraordinarily beneficial. I would love to see a rapid spread of a contagious message of optimum health and wellness. We must recognize that optimal health includes not only physical well-being but mental and spiritual as well. This is why I enthusiastically support the efforts of Al Bacchus and Ace Earp as they launch this program to start a Christian wellness epidemic. Good luck in your journey and may God bless you.

Benjamin Carson, MD
Director of Pediatric Neurosurgery
Professor of Neurological Surgery
Johns Hopkins Medical Institutions &
President and Co-Founder, Carson Scholars Fund
Baltimore, Maryland
July, 2004

Dr. Carson's sentiments connect well with the current social climate.

This quote from the late Congressman John Lewis, who is lying in repose in the Rotunda at the US Capitol Building as I write this on July 27, 2020, is a strong reminder of how the USA (and maybe the world) can again find its ideal in the essence of Christianity.

"At a very early stage of the movement, I accepted the teaching of Jesus, the way of love, the way of nonviolence, the spirit of forgiveness and reconciliation. The idea of hate is too heavy a burden to bear. … I don't want to go down that road. I've seen too much hate, seen too much violence. And I know love is a better way."[14]

I look forward to seeing who will rise to the forefront of the Black Lives Matter movement in the traditions of Martin Luther King, Jr. and Congressman John Lewis.

NOTES FOR YOUR BOOK

_____

_____

_____

_____

_____

_____

_____

_____

_____

_____

_____

_____

_____

_____

13

YOUR BOOK ON LOVE, WELLNESS, AND HAPPINESS

Love is a canvas furnished by nature,
and embroidered by imagination.

—Voltaire

I believe everybody has at least one book in them. Your unique life story is worth sharing, whether you think it will be a best seller or not.

The number one key to writing a book is to be ready. I like the saying, "You've got to be ready when the time is right." To prepare, you have to read and capture. Read, and the mind makes the knowledge and information yours. Then, write down the ideas, questions, and inspirations that arise as you merge new insights with your story.

One formula that works to tell a life story is to do a complete review of your life, show awareness of world and community issues, offer solutions to common problems, and be authentic about your beliefs and motives.

The right time for my first book was 1999. As mentioned in earlier chapters, my wife and I dealt with some unusual circumstances that left us homeless for a few months. Those experiences led me to the Department of Health Education at the University of Maryland, College Park, Maryland, where I was offered the opportunity to create a course for the adult education division, and taught the course for fifteen years.

One day in 1998, I shared the course content with a professional acquaintance who invited me to join him in making a presentation to the owner of an electronics company. This gentleman had a very successful year and was seeking to establish a publishing division. I prepared a Power-Point slide show highlighting my material and mustered my best presentation techniques.

I could hardly believe my ears when the cash-rich business owner said, "I like your stuff. I'll pay you an advance for using your materials. You retain copyright, and I'll hire you at the salary you had at your last job. You can manage the production process. I'll hire a director to manage the business affairs of the publishing section of the company. How much do you want? I'll have the CFO write you a check today."

> THE NUMBER THAT CAME TO MIND WAS $10,000. LOOKING BACK, I SHOULD HAVE SAID $20,000!

As a struggling entrepreneur, I made presentations, waited for call- backs to follow up on interests, and made offers and counteroffers before getting a contract. I was not prepared for a decisive offer from an initial presentation. The number that came to mind was $10,000. "Okay, go to the human resource department and fill out the paperwork, then drop by the business office to pick up your check." Looking back, I should have said $20,000!

That was how the book *Personal Wellness: How to Go the Distance* was born. My wife was co-author, and I hired a physician-writer to be the editor. (Margaret Savage, MD, MPH was the medical director at the Koop Foundation at the time. Yes, *that* C. Everett Koop, a former surgeon general of the USA.[1]) The business paid for publication of 10,000 copies of a 300+ page book with 16 color plates. The $10,000 advance was unencumbered, meaning I never had to pay it back from royalties.

The time was right, and I was prepared. You have been preparing all your life too. Maybe you are not at the stage of readiness you want to be, but you have unique experiences, a personal interpretation of love, wellness, and happiness—or some aspects of those topics—and you feel a desire to help somebody else. The chief aim in writing a book is not to make money. It is about helping other travelers on this road of life to have a more enjoyable journey.

Two things that motivated us to put our notes together for the book were having a picture of the book cover in mind, and having a strong desire to dedicate it to someone who greatly impacted our lives.

o **The Book Cover**
    The idea to use an illustration for a book cover as a wellness promoting device came from the concept of logotherapy, as explained by Viktor Frankl in his book *Man's Search for Meaning*.[2] Drawing pictures help to organize the mind, unravel meaning out of suffering, and stir creativity. The image may change as the book is written, but starting with a concept in mind captures a lot of meaning.

    My wife drew the idea for our book cover free hand. She captured the concepts of a heart positioned at the emotional centers of the brain, supported by the hands, with rays of sunlight pushing back dark clouds.

Our graphics artist, James Arkusinski, composed the computerized version, which can be seen on Amazon.[3]

This illustration has additional meaning as James couldn't find pre-made graphics to represent the hands properly, so he took a photo of his own hands to finish the composition. James has been and still is a very special friend.

o **The Dedication**
The main dedication in that first book was to my parents, Gerald and Enid Bacchus. Looking back, their love story and hard work to raise a family of ten children is simply amazing. Dad had a third-grade education and Mom never went to school, but one strong driving force in their lives was getting an education for their children. They sacrificed to send us all to a private school operated by the church, then to college, mostly in the USA.

Among us siblings, we hold three doctoral, nine masters, ten bachelors, and two nursing degrees. There are four medical doctor degrees, along with various degrees in business, biology, and other professions among all of their grandchildren. One of my treasured pictures of Dad is him dressed in my Michigan State University doctoral regalia.

However, the most precious memory of our parents is how tenderly, patiently, and lovingly Dad cared for Mom in her declining years. After 63 years together, they really had a full life of love, wellness, and happiness. They did the best with what they had. Their cherished dream to have a medical doctor among their children was not realized, but four of their grandchildren made up for that.

I believe the tenderness with which Dad took care of Mom in those final years is a genetic trait. I see it in myself as I care for a wife who has gone through cancer surgery, chemotherapy, radiation treatment, and a mastectomy, only to end up with a major autoimmune condition most of her doctors have never seen. I see it in my brothers and my two sons, especially the second son who gives all of his heart and soul in relationships. And now, I see it in my grandson, William James Alban Bacchus—a fourth generation blessing. One of the best compliments I have ever received was when I introduced a friend to my mother and she said, "He is the tender-hearted one." I can say that proudly of William.

This, my second book, is dedicated to my wife as we celebrate our 50th wedding anniversary.

****

The guidance I gave my students for writing their books in both the Healthier Living (HLSC 110) and Christ-Centered Wellness (HLSC 270) courses was outlined as follows:

o **Do a life review.** Break up your life thus far into seven-year periods. What key events and strong memories come to mind? Sift through the good and the bad. Evaluate what you are comfortable sharing that may help someone else or makes an interesting story. It may trigger a smile, inspiration, or a new thought in someone else. I'll give a few examples from my life, without many details. I'm running out of space in this book, and I prefer to use many of my stories in presentations instead of in the written form. (You may skip this section on my life review. It is given here as an example as you prepare to review your life story. If you have no intention of writing a book, this may be boring!)

- o Birth–7 (1946–1953)
  - One strong memory and regret is being a witness to a new student's humiliation at our school, and not doing anything about it. An older student pulled down the new student's pants during recess. Young boys did not use underwear in those days, and I looked on without objecting. I wish I had the guts back then to stand up for him.
  - I was very self-conscious about being cross-eyed and left-handed. I was very hopeful about getting my eyes straightened when my mother took me to be evaluated by Dr. Gunmonro. He described the surgery needed to tighten one set of external eye muscles. My mother did not agree to the surgery, thinking the risks of my going blind were too high. I tried a covering patch to exercise the weak eye, but that didn't work.

- o 7–14 (1953–1960)
  - At ten years old, I broke my leg and spent three months in the hospital.
  - I came close to killing one of my brothers with a butcher knife in a fit of rage. (That's the brother who has the big scar on his leg.)
  - Urban Antoine was principal when I aced the entrance exam for high school. I remember him for leaving the island the night before his wedding.
  - Pregnant women came to buy groceries from our shop so they could look at my crossed eyes

hoping their child would be born with such a
beautiful look.

- ○ 14–21 (1960–1967)
  - I made the top grades in every class and got the
    highest pass on the Senior Cambridge Exams.
  - This was when I committed the most regretted
    act of my entire life—the incident I described
    earlier with my second girlfriend.
  - During these years, I preached regularly in our
    church. After my first sermon, I felt a strong call
    to evangelistic ministry.
  - At 17, I decided on a name for my first son,
    though he was not born until nine years later.
  - I acted as the lead character in the play "The Life
    of Paul." It was an emotional high to flawlessly
    deliver all the major speeches of St. Paul. (I felt
    ready for Hollywood!)
  - When I left St. Vincent for college at Andrews
    University in Michigan, I lived with my brother
    Rick and his wife Gerzel that first summer.

- ○ 21–28 (1967–1974)
  - At Andrews University, I lived in the men's
    dormitory with my roommate, Cliff Sutherland,
    and our suitemate, Gideon Lewis.
  - In 1968, Gideon and I spent the summer in
    Alberta, Canada, selling books door-to-door and
    creating wonderful friendships.
  - I fell in love and entered an inter-racial marriage,
    and learned many lessons that came with that
    adventure.
  - I graduated with a medical technology degree,
    and our first son was born when I was 26.

- The day we brought our first-born home from the hospital, we picked a name for our second son.
- My wife suffered a miscarriage and nearly bled to death.
- I received a master's degree in biology, and our second son was born when I was 28 years old.
- We moved to East Lansing, Michigan, so I could pursue doctoral studies in human physiology at Michigan State University.

- 28–35 (1974–1981)
  - I became a US citizen in 1976. The bicentennial celebrations were memorable with a traveling show "The Spirit of '76," held at major stadiums around the country.
  - I worked a midnight to 7:00 a.m. shift on weekends at a hospital lab while doing fulltime doctoral studies.
  - I got to appreciate the rigors of training as a research scientist.
  - Our daughter was born at the beginning of the same year I wrote my doctoral dissertation. My wife had the name for a daughter in mind since she was a teenager.
  - I missed my doctoral graduation ceremony because it was held on Sabbath—a major regret.
  - We moved to Charlottesville, Virginia, to serve a post-doc fellowship in the lab of Dr. Robert M Berne at the University of Virginia (UVA).[4] Though I felt I had science research in my future, I discovered that the rigors of such a life were too stressful for me. (I still feel proud of having a paper in the *American Journal of Physiology* with Doctors Ely, Rubio, and Berne as co-authors.

When we visit our granddaughter, Lauren, while she attends UVA, I plan to tour the cardiovascular research center named in Dr. Berne's honor.)

- I found the limits of my abilities to cope with the demands of being a research scientist, and settled for college teaching. We moved to Takoma Park, Maryland, in 1981, experienced the particularly difficult winter of 1982, and retain a strong memory of the Air Florida plane crash into the icy Potomac River.

- 35–42 (1981–1988)
  - We found out the difference between chapter 7 and chapter 11 bankruptcy.
  - I connected with the Department of Health Education at the University of Maryland and got to create the course "Personal Wellness and Self-realization."
  - We were adopted into the Southern Asian Community of the Maryland-Washington, DC area, and have great memories of caring support and friendships from this social group. Robinson and Vimala Abraham were instrumental in anchoring those relationships, and their many acts of kindness and generosity are treasured memories.
  - I obtained a job with the cardiac surgeons at Washington Hospital Center as research director and assistant administrator.
  - They also hired my wife to coordinate a computerized database for coronary bypass and valve replacement patients.
  - We formed a company I named Total Health, Inc. so my wife could do the same work but with

the flexibility of setting her hours and working from home.

- o 42–49 (1988–1995)
  - We invited a single, teenage mother and her two-month-old son to live with us, and created great memories for the whole family.
  - I took Life Coach training and got involved in coaching activities and workshops in the Washington, DC area, at government offices and private corporations.
  - Our first son graduated from high school. (He insisted his diploma had his full name, and all his names be read without abbreviations at the graduation ceremony. Along with Michael Fitzgerald, which I had chosen since I was 17 years old, my wife wanted a connection to my Indian heritage, so we had named him Michael Fitzgerald Rhambullocksingh Bacchus—all but six letters of the alphabet!)

- o 49–56 (1995–2002)
  - I met the guy who introduced me to the CEO of the company who cut a same-day check for $10,000 and published my first book.
  - After resigning from a stable job which had become unfulfilling, I took my retirement account and tried to establish a health education and data management business.
  - My start-up publishing company failed in the aftermath of the burst dot com bubble.
  - After two major contracts for health education products worth $150K (a stop-smoking module for Florida Hospital/Celebration Health and

a Wellness Coaching course for Montgomery College, Maryland), I realized a one-person company was not viable. It consumed too much time and effort to market services. While fulfilling a contract, there's no time for marketing, and a dry spell can wipe you out.

- 56–63 (2002–2009)
  - In a rather unusual way, I got back into college teaching. The college needed an athletic director to fill in for a year while the person hired finished up elsewhere. I got the interim position, which led to full-time teaching for another eight years.
  - My final years of teaching included "Human Anatomy and Physiology," "Healthier Living," "Fitness & Wellness," and "Exercise Physiology."
  - When given the opportunity to develop a new course, I titled it "Christ-Centered Wellness."
  - I got three articles published in *Adventist Review*, and won an international competition for a sermon on a health education model, CELEBRATIONS.
  - I formed a company, Wellness Unlimited, LLC, to distribute my workbook for "Christ-Centered Wellness," and conducted workshops on the theme.
  - This was the most enjoyable stretch of my career. I got to teach what I loved, was allowed creative control of a few courses, sold workbooks to the university bookstore, and played lots of racquetball and ping-pong with the students. (I preferred to spend time with my students instead of attending faculty and administrative meetings as I had no ambitions for administration.)

- o 63–70 (2009–2016)
  - Because of a generous salary offer (a 50% raise), I took a one-year break from teaching to serve as Vice-President for Academic Affairs at a private college. It confirmed the reasons I avoided administration.
  - I went back to college teaching the next year. Then, an inexperienced department chair promised me a continuation of my faculty role in the department but selected someone else for the position. (He got booted out within a couple years after that.) So, I retired in 2011, eligible for social security and Medicare.
  - Unfortunately, I experienced what many people go through with the cancer diagnosis of a loved one, and the treatment process.
  - My wife and I comfortably discussed the reality of having only a few years left, and decided to make the most of it.

- o 70–74 (2016–2020)
  - The most memorable birthday celebration of my life was my 70th birthday. I taught part-time, and one of my students was pregnant. I felt inspired to dedicate my 70th birthday celebration to helping this single mother prepare for the arrival of twin boys. My family enthusiastically organized an all-day open house, and cooked Caribbean dishes. A huge group of friends including my pickleball buddies attended and contributed enough to purchase a reliable used car for the young lady— the exact thing for which she was hoping and praying.

- Two days before this party, I had one of the biggest surprises of my entire life—the birth of a second grandson, weighing in at one pound and nine ounces.

- We started checking off major bucket list items such as fulfilling a promise I had made to my wife during our courtship to take her to Banff National Park in Canada. It was an exciting road-trip from Martinsburg, West Virginia, to Banff in Alberta in the summer of 2017. During this trip, I reconnected with Hazel Thomsen, the mother of the family who befriended my cousin and me in 1968, when we were selling books in Rocky Mountain House. She was planning her "Alive and Kicking" funeral service. She said, "I want you to attend and sing that duet you did with your cousin when you were here 49 years ago!" So, I got my cousin, Dr. Gideon Lewis, to join me in getting to Rocky Mountain House two months later, Labor Day weekend, 2017. What a beautiful funeral service with the person right there, alive, enjoying it, and taking part. We sang our duet "Back of the Clouds." The reception dinner following the service was elegant with a memorable life history delivered with quirky humor. She died five months later. We went back for the scattering of her ashes, Labor Day weekend of 2018.

- The "Alive and Kicking" funeral service above inspired me to suggest to my cousins that we organize celebrations for our elders while they are still able to enjoy them. An in-person event for 2019 did not materialize. Then came PN-20. The perfect answer to the logistics was a Zoom conference. Thanks to the technical expertise of my younger cousins, we pulled off the first one on July 11, 2020. The honoree, Uncle Vertyl (author of the proverb on the Part 3 fly page of this book), at 97 years of age, enjoyed the program with 80 attendees in several countries including Canada, the USA, Turkey, the UK, and St. Vincent. We plan to do more and expand beyond relatives to church family and friends.

- o Beyond 2020
  If PN-20 had not changed our plans, this book would not have been written this year, or maybe never! We had an all-summer travel itinerary set but had to cancel. After canceling reservations for hot-air ballooning over Sedona, Arizona, visits to Death Valley and Yosemite National Parks, and a three-day stay at Lake Tahoe, California, there was a huge void in my life. With no NCAA basketball (I believe my Spartans of Michigan State had a chance for the title), I lost interest in TV programs. Now, I find writing more fun than watching TV. I plan to continue writing as I believe I have several books in me.

I hope after a treatment and a vaccine are in place for CV-19, we can pick up our travel plans. Our second son is very excited about the hiking scenery in the pacific northwest as he moved to Oregon. We plan to spend a month out there, while we are still able to, and take in Crater Lake, Mount Hood, and all the other gorgeous sites. Then, we'll make our last trip to Banff and Jasper in Alberta.

Our bucket list is long. We plan to visit St. Vincent for my 75th birthday and the celebration of Indian Arrival Day. Tentatively, we have a trip with our grandchildren on the schedule for December 2021 to sail between St. Vincent and Grenada. I have never visited the Grenadines beyond Bequia. Our 17-year-old grandson, William, is certified to captain for a 45ft double-hull sailboat, so we look forward to a new adventure.

> I HOPE AS YOU REVIEW YOUR LIFE YOU WILL FIND JOY IN YOUR PAST, SATISFACTION IN YOUR PRESENT, AND ANTICIPATED PLEASURE IN YOUR FUTURE.

I hope as you review your life, you will find joy in your past, satisfaction in your present, and anticipated pleasure for the future; contentment for today is a major key to happiness.

****

The other requirement in the book project for my classes was a review of beliefs and values. In doing this, you see how your core beliefs have affected your life, and how they may have changed. Most of my students in the last five years of teaching were no older than 30. Yet, they had some significant adjustments to make when reconciling what they were taught at home and in church, with what they were experiencing in real life.

I usually share how my beliefs affected my life in seven areas and how I have adjusted those beliefs. In my opinion, spiritual growth continues till we die. I view the seven areas below as the items which fuel my spiritual growth in this last segment of my life.

1. The Shortness of Time

As I discussed earlier, I grew up strongly indoctrinated with the idea the end of the world was so near I may not reach adulthood. As a lay preacher at 18 years old, I did one sermon on the age of Earth. I repeated what I learned and predicted that the world would end before the year 2000.

As a consequence of this belief, I did not have a long-range plan for my life. I went through the growth stages from childhood to older adult, but something was missing. For one, I did not plan for retirement. The adjustment I had to make is evident in leading my students in constructing "A Prosperity Plan" as part of their coursework in "Christ-centered Wellness." And of course, trying to catch up with retirement preparedness. I continue to work part-time teaching online biology courses well into my retirement years. (The extra income is great to fund our travels, and the intellectual stimulation is good anti-aging medicine.)

2. The Love of Money

I bought in so strongly to the beliefs found in 1 Timothy 6:10 about the love of money being the root of all evil, and James 5:1 about rich men weeping and howling because of miseries, that as a teenager, I decided I would settle for just enough to get by. Now, I advise my students and coaching clients to optimize their earning potential. Don't let the chase for riches be the driving force to over-stress your life, but explore all legitimate ways to generate income. The more you have, the greater good you can do. It is a pleasant experience to be with relatives and friends who have optimized their earning capabilities and are kind and generous with their excess resources.

One year ago, I thought I should experience what it felt like to invest in the stock market. It was thrilling to see a 30% increase in one year—till it all disappeared in the crash caused by PN-20! I did follow the maxim to "not gamble more than you can afford to lose." Then, it all came back only to disappear again! Now, my attitude is if it goes, it goes; if it returns, it returns. I hear stories from my peers who bought stocks in Apple and Amazon when they were sold under $50 per share. I accept my missing out because I understand my reasons. Midway through the second month of 2021, my stock shot up to 80% gain. Maybe, I'm on to something good—the next Apple?

I usually advise my students and clients that $75K US annual income is a good minimum goal for a single person, and you need two of those to raise a family comfortably these days in the USA.

3. **The Age of the Earth**
The first concept I had of the age of the earth was established in grade school. The textbook we used had a table showing the year of creation of Earth as 4004 BC. So, if a 6000-year limit was the predicted duration of time on earth (as our church literature promoted), then it should end before 2000 A.D. Then the scientists within the church added a few thousand years to make the earth approximately 10,000 years old.

As I studied geologic formations, and the scientific dating methods, I rationalized that Earth's core and mantle could be all those millions of years old, but the topography was a recent creation. In my beliefs, all major geologic formations were explained by Noah's flood.

In my recent visits to the Grand Canyon, the Grand Tetons, Yellowstone National Park, the Painted Desert, and Petrified Forest National Park in Arizona, these questions came to mind: Did God create these? Did Noah's flood create these? If Earth is made new someday, will these hard-to-get places remain? Suppose I can fly someday, won't it be lovely to explore these places just as they are but on wings as an eagle?

Recently, I had some additional thoughts and questions on this topic after perusing a webpage "BioLogos—God's Word, God's World."[5] I believe during PN-20, everybody has heard of Dr. Anthony Fauci, the director of the National Institute of Allergy and Infectious Diseases at the National Institutes of Health (NIH) in the USA. I read some of his work and background and noticed that his boss, Dr. Francis Collins, the director of the NIH, had a foundation named BioLogos: "Bio" for life, and "Logos" for Word of God. The goal of BioLogos is to show how the Christian faith is compatible with science.

After my first perusal of the website, I became sure that I wanted to be a part of this conversation. The expert theologians and scientists whose discussions I have read so far seem to reconcile Earth's age (billions of years) with creation by God. They offer a very long period of time for creation week, using the days as symbolic of evolutionary time periods. The first question that raised for me is about the seventh-day Sabbath. I grew up with a strong belief in a 24-hour day during creation week with a holy seventh day when God rested. I look forward to hanging out with this group of scientists for a while and see what I learn and what new questions may arise. I believe in a God who loves discussions and questions and who encourages exploration. So happy for that freedom!

4. **The Role of the United States in End-of-the-World Events**
The church that formed my early beliefs and concepts about the end of the world was very big on prophecy and

end-times events. Teachings emphasized the prophecies of Daniel and the events described in the book of Revelation. Interpretations of these prophecies led to a prediction that the United States will play a major role in the events at the end of the world.

A major part of the prediction was the principles of the US Constitution would be set aside, and some form of a radical, non-democratic government will prevail. There would be a National Sunday Law, and a small group of seventh-day Sabbath-keepers would be forced to comply or face persecution.

For most of my adult life, I have had a difficult time trying to envision how that prediction may actually happen. I became a US citizen in 1976 and have been a casual observer of government and politics but never took the time to study in-depth. I believed the checks and balances in government would never allow for any semblance of a dictatorship to take hold.

Well, until January 6, 2021, when a large crowd of angry rioters stormed the US Capitol Building and disrupted a joint session of congress.[6] I can now see how it's possible. We could easily have tumbled into a "banana republic" experience if a greater strategic plan were in place. If the president-elect and members of Congress had been arrested and jailed, and if the military enforced the wishes of the outgoing president, a dictatorship could have been established. This history-making event, in the country which is the world's leader for encouraging the spread of democratic forms of government, has stirred my interest in diligently restudying and reexamining my end-of-the-world beliefs.

5. Politics in the USA

When I learned the subject of "civics" in elementary school, the major idea that stood out was opposing parties in a democracy competed fiercely but fairly in elections. However, once the elections ended, both parties look to how they can contribute to building up the nation before the next election.

Currently in the USA, I see such strong polarization between two parties that there is little or no cooperation for the common good. Politicians give the impression that their greatest goal is to protect their position and office instead of the common good. Will this ever change? Maybe it will, with a new generation of leaders whose ideals are rooted in the concepts of love, truth, and decency toward all human beings.

I hold myself as an Independent and have voted both ways in past elections. What I look for in a leader are more positive qualities than negative qualities.

We all have faults. But a leader has to rise above his personal faults and unscientific impulses, and be a unifier, a forgiver, a promoter, and a visionary for the common good.

6. The Black Lives Matter Movement

I don't have any wisdom to share on the Black Lives Matter movement. In my view, it is the continuation of the work of the Civil Rights Movement, and the legacy of those leaders, especially Martin Luther King, Jr., and Congressman John Lewis. As such, the ideal of non-violent protests must continue to guide activities. I see this movement growing in their tradition with a lot of music—gospel, spirituals, hymns, and new compositions. It would be great if a pastor/musician would lead a huge choir as an integral part of the movement. Maybe that's already in the vision. Right now, I don't feel safe enough or young enough to join protest marches. I believe young leaders and the millennial generation are ready to take on this moment to continue the peaceful struggle for equal rights for all.

I'll let these words of Rep John Lewis, from an interview with PBS in 2004, carry the sentiments that I believe will lead this movement to accomplish its goals in the same spirit of "Satyagraha," and the Gospel of Jesus Christ that fueled India's independence marches and the Civil Rights Movement.[7,8]

> *At a very early stage of the movement, I accepted the teaching of Jesus, the way of love, the way of nonviolence, the spirit of forgiveness and reconciliation. The idea of hate is too heavy a burden to bear. … I don't want to go down that road. I've seen too much hate, seen too much violence. And I know love is a better way.*

> *We studied the great religions of the world. We discussed and debated the teachings of the great teacher. And we would ask questions about what would Jesus do. In preparing for the sit-ins, we felt that the message was one of love—the message of love in action: don't hate. If someone hits you, don't strike back. Just turn the other side. Be prepared to forgive. That's not anything any Constitution say anything about forgiveness. It is straight from the Scripture: reconciliation. So the movement, the early foundation, the early teaching of the movement was based on the Scripture, the teaching*

of Jesus, the teaching of Gandhi and others. You have to remind people over and over again that some of us saw our involvement in the civil rights movement as an extension of our faith.

On many occasions, people would be so inspired, so moved ... they would start singing some of the gospel songs or some hymn of the church. And they would improvise; they would make it current, or make it so powerful, that you knew somehow and some way that you had to go. You had to go and sit in. You had to go and march, because it was the power of the message, of the words of a song—the beat, the rhythm. And on some occasions, it was just like being in church on a Sunday morning. It was like being at a prayer meeting. And whether it was a sit-in, or whether it was on the freedom ride, or the march from Selma to Montgomery, I felt on many occasions like it was a very deep religious experience.

The quote above loses its impact when you try to paraphrase or dissect. It reveals the depth of thought, beliefs, struggle, and commitment of a man of courage speaking from the heart.

Then, the quotes from his essay that was published in the New York Times on July 30, 2020, the day of his funeral.[9]

Though I may not be here with you, I urge you to answer the highest calling of your heart and stand up for what you truly believe. In my life I have done all I can to demonstrate that the way of peace, the way of love and nonviolence is the more excellent way. Now it is your turn to let freedom ring.

> *When historians pick up their pens to write the story of*
> *the 21st century, let them say that it was your generation*
> *who laid down the heavy burdens of hate at last and*
> *that peace finally triumphed over violence, aggression*
> *and war. So, I say to you, walk with the wind, brothers*
> *and sisters, and let the spirit of peace and the power of*
> *everlasting love be your guide.*

I hope these thoughts from a man who lived his beliefs will guide all revolutionary movements in this country.

7. Providential Guidance

At 21 years of age, I played a mind-game with my beliefs in God's guidance. Since I was 17 years old, I was convinced I was destined to be a pastor/evangelist. I had bargained with God thus: "If You help me to get the highest pass on the Senior Cambridge Exams, I'll use that as the indicator I should follow the path of the pastor/evangelist. If I get anything less than the highest pass, I will follow the wishes of my mother to become a medical doctor." Maybe I was even trying to manipulate God at that time! I entered college at 21 and enrolled in a pre-med curriculum to please my mother rather than honor my bargain with God. I think family pride and personal prestige were stronger influences than a four-year-old promise to God.

However, as I review my life several years later, I believe all of it was part of God's plan for my life. He knew I would make the decisions I made at 21, knew ahead of time where I would be most effective in my work, and what would be best for my life's contribution. I am happy with the outcome—a career experimenting with different aspects of life, developing and sharing a unique perspective of blending science, psychology and religion into a practical approach to life. It has been a blessing to have had many experiences—a medical technologist, a research physiologist, a biology professor, a wellness coach, an entrepreneur, an educator, a good father, a husband of one wife for 50 years, a decent friend, and overall good person. I have many faults, but I seek to continue growing, and building more positives to choke out the negatives. I've had more pleasure than pain in this life and still hold that God leads our lives, if we so believe.

As I write this on August 5, 2020, the day before our 50th anniversary, I only have to review how Carol and I met and grew together, to reinforce the belief of God's leading in our lives. We grew up in similar religious cultures but in different countries—she in a midwestern state in the USA, and I in a village on the Caribbean island of St. Vincent. We met by coincidence one midnight on the campus of Andrews University in Berrien Springs, Michigan.

I was the midnight to 3:00 a.m. watchman on campus, and she was the midnight to 4:00 a.m. switchboard operator in the women's dormitory. One of my tasks was to go to the women's dorm, clock in at the west entrance, pick up the mail from her, and clock out at the east exit on the way to the post office.

In our casual, nightly interaction, I noticed she didn't have the white-girl superiority I thought would be there. (I grew up with expectations from parents and myself to marry an Indian girl.) We exchanged pleasantries for several weeks before I suggested we attend a church program together. We did, and after that, started spending the hour between the end of my shift and the end of hers on the phone—in buildings on opposite ends campus.

We discussed the social implications of being seen around campus together. Her parents had strong expectations of her avoiding non-white social attention. We decided our relationship should not progress. Our last church "date" was a Friday night vesper. We sat in the balcony level. As we started to leave, she slipped and sprained an ankle and had to use crutches for three weeks. I couldn't break off our friendship then—she needed help with getting to class on crutches. I walked her to classes and carried her books.

As we approached the Christmas holidays, we had what I thought was a final conversation about our inter-racial friendship. We decided to break it off as she was going home to Illinois, and I was staying in Michigan to work on campus.

I was late for work one night and took a bicycle to the building to clock in. I did not expect ice on the sidewalk in early December. My bike slipped on the ice, and I broke an ankle. As a result, I was unable to work, and could not stay in the dormitory with no income.

My cousin offered to let me stay with him in an apartment in Illinois, where he was doing his internship in medical technology. It just so happened that he lived one block away from where Carol lived. I didn't have a phone number to contact her, so I just walked up to her front-door—on crutches. That did it. Maybe, I looked so pathetic that it stirred more than the friendship we had broken a week before. Maybe it was inspiration. Whatever it was, things clicked, and we dated seriously the next semester in college. And the rest is our history. We got married before knowing each other for a full year. She went back to work as an x-ray tech, and I continued my medical technology training. She dropped out of college, and I returned to finish my senior year. Our first son was born the summer after I graduated, just shy of three years after we first met.

The rest of our adventure took us to Michigan State University, the University of Virginia, Columbia Union College (now Washington Adventist University), and the University of Maryland. We felt safe at institutions of higher learning. Our three children have not had any major negative experiences based on their inter-racial heritage. In fact, they received attention for their complexion and physical features.

As we review our 50 years together, we conclude God led. We faced the world with a united front and had fun. We overcame major hurdles, and we would do it all over again, together.

And I believe Providential guidance made me ready to write *Love, Wellness, and Happiness* at this particular time in Earth's history. What do you believe about your life and solutions to major societal problems?

NOTES FOR YOUR BOOK

14

FINAL REFLECTIONS ON LOVE, WELLNESS, AND HAPPINESS

Love is of all passions the strongest, for it attacks
simultaneously the head, the heart, and the senses.

—Lao Tzu

In this book, I have offered a unique synthesis of knowledge, principles, practices, beliefs, values, and experiences that lead to a happy, fulfilled life. Love must be the foundation. Understanding love and practicing love as Christ taught and modelled would lead us to resolve all the problems of race, caste, economics, politics, governance, safety, and resource needs. Happiness is the product of living, guided by love.

You can regulate your daily attitude to make yourself happy even as the ups and downs of life challenge that happiness. Wellness practices and stress management techniques are useful, but they don't bring happiness. Optimizing your income helps but also does not bring happiness. Loving and

> HAPPINESS IS THE PRODUCT OF LIVING, GUIDED BY LOVE.

serving, however, do bring fulfillment and happiness. Each individual evaluates how and when they are happy and fulfilled. It is a daily assertion when you are doing your best with what you have.

As I journey through my 75th year of life, I can honestly say I have studied many religious and philosophical teachings. I have read health and wellness literature, books on self-help strategies, teachings of the great world religions, and writings by leaders of philosophical thought such as the Dalai Lama. I also love connecting with current researchers and thought leaders at major institutions of higher learning.

Such memorable connections include Harold Koenig, MD, Director, Center for Spirituality, Theology and Health at Duke University. His book *The Healing Power of Faith: Science Explores Medicine's Last Great Frontier* was influential in structuring my course content for "Christ-Centered Wellness." It was even more influential to spend a week in his research methods workshop and witness his humility, the genuine practice of the principles he taught, and his love and care for everyone in the group.

I have yet to find inspiration more direct and simplified than what Christ taught and lived according to the Gospel stories. And I've yet to find better descriptions of the way to happiness, love, and well-being than what the disciples of Christ wrote. It could be my early indoctrination in Christianity was so strong, that nothing else can have more meaning. Old Testament passages also have lessons on these topics.[1]

Let's review a few of these statements that directly apply to love, wellness, and happiness.

- **Peace**
  - From childhood, I memorized Scripture passages as a part of the weekly routine in church and school. Since my early teens, my favorite passage of Scripture has been John 14:27. "Peace I leave with you, my peace I give to you. Not as the world gives do I give to you. Let not your hearts be troubled, neither let them be afraid." I have used this as a stress resistance device throughout my life. Then, after I learned the well-researched relaxation technique publicized by Dr. Herbert Benson of Harvard University, I used "peace" as my repeated word matching with my breathing. (See Appendix I for The Relaxation Response.)

- **Happiness**
  - Christ's teachings in one of His first sermons used the word "blessed" many times. The Young's Literal Translation renders the verses of Matthew 5 with the word blessed replaced by happy. "Happy the poor in spirit, because . . . Happy the mourning, because . . . Happy the meek, because . . . Happy the peacemakers, because . . .
  I like this version as it carries the idea of experiencing something, instead of being pronounced as commended or consecrated.

  - This one needs no further comment. Isaiah 52:7 says, "How beautiful upon the mountains are the feet of him who brings good news, who publishes peace, who brings good news of happiness, who publishes salvation, who says to Zion, "Your God reigns."

o **Love**
  o It's challenging to select from so many. I think the best known is the writings of St. Paul in 1 Corinthians 13, which is quoted or paraphrased at most Christian weddings. I'll paraphrase the New King James Version (NKJV) here:

  - Even if I speak several languages, earthly or heavenly, and cannot love, I'm only a chatterbox making useless noises.
  - Even if I have supernatural knowledge and powers, and can perform miracles, but do not have love, I am nothing.
  - Even if I give away all that I own to help the poor, and even if I am burned at the stake for what I believe, but do not have love, I gain nothing.
  - Love is patient, kind, not envious, does not boast or make a show.
  - Love is not rude, selfish, hot-tempered, nor willfully evil.
  - Love does not find joy in doing bad, hurtful things to people.
  - Love finds joy in the truth.
  - Love puts up with many things, believes what the loved one says, always hopes for the best, and endures for a lifetime.
  - Love never fails. Humans may fail but love is enduring.
  - Faith, hope, and love are three pillars of life, but love is the most important one.

  o "Greater love has no one than this, than to lay down one's life for his friends" (John 15:13).

- o "There is no fear in love, but perfect love casts out fear . . . If someone says "I love God," and hates his brother, he is a liar" (1 John 4:18, 20).
- o "Let love be without hypocrisy. Abhor what is evil. Cling to what is good. Be kindly affectionate to one another with brotherly love, in honor giving preference to one another" (Romans 12:9 & 10, NKJV).

- o **Faith**
  - o I define faith as believing in ideas that cannot be tested by the scientific method. This includes God, miracles such as bringing dead people back to life, and a future existence in a perfect world.
  - o Without faith, there is no Christianity. If science can prove that Jesus Christ was not raised from the dead, then the whole foundation of the Christian faith crumbles.
  - o Romans 1:17 tells us, "For in it the righteousness of God is revealed from faith to faith; as it is written, 'The just shall live by faith.'"
  - o "Now faith is the substance of things hoped for, the evidence of things not seen" (Hebrews 11:1).

- o **Hope**
  - o Humans have the capacity to anticipate the future and consciously prepare for it. Research shows people who live with an optimistic outlook enjoy life more, have better health, and live longer.[2]
  - o Sometimes, Christians are accused of living with unrealistic hopes about a future perfect world. This "pie-in-the-sky-by-and-by" designation is used as ridicule of the unscientific beliefs about sudden, cataclysmic ending of "a sinful world" to be replaced

by a new, sinless creation. The certainty for believers is grounded on faith that what the Bible says is true. From there, the strength of faith keeps hope alive.

o   Apart from the major hope of a re-created world, Christians live like everybody else in this present world where hope for a better future is a healthy and health-promoting attitude. Most humans hope things will get better; they hope their children will have a more comfortable life than the parents did, that each succeeding generation will achieve more than the last, and that good will triumph over bad. Hope for the better is a good thing.

o   Hebrews 6:19 tells us, "This hope we have as an anchor of the soul, both sure and steadfast . . ." (See also: Romans 8:18–25 and Ephesians 4:11–16.)

o   **Joy**
  o   I define joy as surges of happiness that may be brief, short-term or long-term. When joy becomes long-term, it raises the baseline of happiness.

  o   "You will show me the path of life;
  In Your presence is fullness of joy;
  At Your right hand are pleasures forevermore"
  (Psalm 16:11).

  o   "So, they went out quickly from the tomb with fear and great joy, and ran to bring His disciples word" (Matt 28: 8). This mixture of fear and great joy challenges my emotional imagination.

  o   "And there was great joy in that city" (Acts 8:8). This makes me wonder what it takes to have great joy in my city, my community, my nation, and my world.

- o **Wellness**
  - o My "Christ-Centered Wellness" philosophy was inspired by the text and context of 3 John 2 which says, "Beloved, I pray that you may prosper in all things and be in health, just as your soul prospers." From that, I combined wellness of body and soul with prosperity. It seemed wellness of the soul is the top priority, and the most readily available.
  - o Among my college students, I found most of them were still uncertain about their beliefs about life after this life and how that can be a certainty.
  - o If you have not yet read "10 Health Principles for Body and Soul," now is a good time to peruse it.[3]

I believe if I were raised in Hinduism (part of my Indian heritage), I would have been a good Hindu. If I were raised in the Jewish or Catholic religions, I would have been a good Jew, or a good Catholic. And if I were raised as an atheist, I would have been a good atheist. However, I was raised in a Protestant Christian system that exuded evangelistic fervor. I believe I have grown and moderated some of the system's extreme beliefs and practices, while maintaining the core foundation.

Since that is what has guided my journey, my philosophy of life, my relationship with my neighbors, my sense of world citizenship and my hopes for the future, that is what I can recommend without reservation.

The path to happiness is to let your core beliefs lead. Assert your daily happiness supported by wellness practices (see Appendix I). Live by the chief guiding principle of love to all. Be a citizen of the world and serve humanity. When you put love at the foundation of a life with grace, the fruit of the Spirit, being parts of one body, and serving one another with no distinction over gender or ethnicity, you cannot help but come up happy and well.

High level wellness is fulfillment regardless of the state of the physical body.

****

In getting this book published, I enrolled in a program led by a master coach. He introduced us to the concept of composing an OPUS. OPUS is an acronym for Overarching Vision, Purpose, Unifying Strategies, and Scorecard for Significance. Here's what I came up with after going through the exercise.

MY OPUS

o **Overarching Vision**
For the rest of my life, I see myself involved in the purposeful planning of experiences that help people to grow to maturity in Christ. Through conversations with individuals, small and large group discussions, in-person or online, I see myself promoting the practical applications of Christ-centered love, wellness, and happiness.

o **Purpose**
My highest purpose is to lift up Christ in my life and encourage others to do the same. The spirit, approach, methods, and treatment of people as demonstrated in the life of Christ, are the most effective methods to help people experience more love, wellness, and happiness.

o **Unifying Strategies**
o Personal growth: I will continue to examine my life for growth areas, and purposefully cultivate the positive qualities of my inner Warrior, Miracle-Worker, Lover, and Ruler.

- o Writing: I will continue to write and plan the dissemination of my written products to benefit my audience and encourage and help others get their writings published.
- o Support Humanitarian Projects: I will plan to contribute time, energy, and finances to humanitarian, educational and healthcare projects where I see it can make a difference. I will help design fundraising activities and events to further these causes.
- o Form Partnerships: I will partner with like-minded souls to contribute to our mutual goals, and complete humanitarian projects.
- o Facilitate Transformational Experiences: I will offer my advice in one-on-one or group experiences to help move people along the path of their vision and goals.
- o Extra-curricular Activities: I will plan deliberate acts of kindness, forgiveness, and celebration for those who need them.

- o **Scorecard of Significance**
  - o I will know I am successful when the following things listed below manifest in my life.
  - o Personal Growth: My family, friends, clients, and associates will see growth in the positive qualities of the Warrior, Miracle-Worker, Lover, and Ruler.
  - o Synergistic Partnerships: I have successful relationships with my peers, a mentor, and clients, especially younger people who want to carry on a program for promoting Christ-Centered Wellness.
  - o Transformative Experiences: I conduct in-person (when feasible), and online experiences for people who wish to promote love, wellness, and happiness within their local communities.

o Compelling Resources: I create written, video, and audio products that promote Christ-Centered Wellness and growth to maturity in Christ.
o Compounding Influence: I will collaborate with other like-mind persons in coaching, team building, and masterminding for sharing practical applications of love, wellness, and happiness.

Well, there you have it! I have poured out my heart and my deepest convictions in a treatise I feel compelled to write. I hope it connects with your journey through life.

****

On August 6, 2020, my wife and I celebrated our 50th wedding anniversary. We have a lot to be thankful for, a lot of fun memories, and a lot that make us proud—good pride. At around four o'clock that morning, I tuned in to a live-streamed funeral service in Hosur, India, for the wife of a friend I admire greatly. This couple (both in their 90s) had a life of great service to humanity.

In 1989, they established Community Uplift Projects (CUP) International, a non-profit organization that was the support channel for Anantha Ashram, in Hosur. The project's goals were to rescue and raise abandoned children—especially baby girls who were discarded— establish a clinic, an orphanage, and educational programs for its residents. I was on the advisory board of CUP International in 1989.

It is a thrill to see what this couple accomplished in 31 years after retirement. They realized every segment of their vision.

Thank you, Sam Uncle and Maggie Aunty for the great example of a life of Christ-like service, with love, wellness, and happiness. I hope my life may contribute such service in this last stretch of the journey.

****

If I leave you with only the current version of my OPUS, and a wonderful example of humanitarian service in the post-retirement years, I would have short-changed you on the subject of growing to maturity in Christ. I would rather leave you with thoughts about motivation and inspiration to live the life you believe uplifts and shares Christ as the ideal in love, wellness, and happiness.

The disciples of Christ, a small group, were intellectually, emotionally, and spiritually charged for action. Having been baptized with the Holy Spirit, they couldn't help but share what inspired them. They had what Malcolm Gladwell would call "a sticky message."[4] Witnesses to the greatest miracle imaginable—a crucified leader raised from the dead—their lives dramatically transformed. They devoted their entire existence to sharing that good news and helping one another. Their main reason for living was to share that good news. They started in their hometown and then travelled to all parts of the known world.

As Gladwell would say, they triggered a positive epidemic. For that to happen, they had the right message, a fully aroused small group, and the right context.

So, my dear reader, the challenge I leave with you is this: as Christians in a post-modern world, do we have a sticky message? Do we have small groups of people fully aroused to the exciting possibilities of that message? Do world issues provide the right context? If our answers are yes, yes, and yes, we should take more concerted action.

The message is by God's grace and the empowerment of the Holy Spirit, we can grow to greater maturity in Christ. The abiding righteousness of Christ transforms lives and meets human needs. We can start and propagate a positive epidemic that changes the world.[5] If we get emotionally charged with the right knowledge, and if we proceed with boldness, we can combine the scientific method, psychology, and Scripture into actionable principles for living. We can be instruments for a transformed world.

The power for that change does not come from any human being. The energy, the vision, the action-plan comes from the characteristics, life, resurrection, and mission of Christ.

He is the Conquering Warrior as we see in Revelation 12:7–11. The battle is won, and there is salvation, and strength, and power. He leads the fight as He did in the deliverance of the Israelites at the Red Sea. "The Lord himself will fight for you. Just stay calm" (Exodus 14:14, NLT).

He is the proven Miracle-worker (John 14:12–21): the humanly impossible is possible, and there is love, and peace.

He is the greatest Lover (John 15:1–17): no greater love than to lay down life, love one another.

He is the coming King (Revelation 19:1–16), Lord God Omnipotent, The Word of God, Faithful, True, Lamb of God, King of Kings and Lord of Lords.

Let's Lift Him Up!

****

The fuel for transformational action is emotions—conviction being a strong emotion. No major change in personal or societal behavior takes place without passion, strong belief, heightened arousal, bold steps, and many times going against the grain. Sometimes, the emotional side is not visible and sometimes when we think it's the win of the intellectual argument, the conviction from the empirical evidence, or the weight of the data, emotions make the difference.

One interesting exercise we do in small groups is to share experiences that recount our emotional highs and lows. Of course, I caution group members to share only those they are comfortable with others knowing. Our past emotional experiences are indicators of the range of our emotional capacity. As a reminder for such interaction and as encouragement for this self-exploration, I share examples of my emotional lows and highs in Appendix 2. This ties in with the "happiness activity" of savoring (Appendix 1).

On April 9, 2021, I turned in my final manuscript to the publishers. That same day, the volcano on the island of St. Vincent (where I grew up), erupted with a succession of three violent explosions. It caused me to think of changing my terminology from "an epidemic of Christ-centered Wellness" to "a series of explosions of Christ-centered Wellness." The world needs Christians to be explosively contagious with a sticky message grounded in love.

RECOMMENDED ACTIONS:

After reading this book, be inspired to take action. Whether you are a Christian or not, growth in love, wellness, and happiness requires you to act. Reading only for enjoyment is not the best use of your time and energy. Here are some action items you may consider:

o   Write your OPUS.
o   Make a list of your emotional highs and lows.
o   Make a list of three to seven things in your life you want to change.
o   Rate the items above in order of priority.
o   Begin with your highest priority and set goals to make the change you want.
o   Tell your family and/or friends what you are working on.

o Enlist at least one person to hold you accountable for acting on your plan.
o Set a date to put your plan into action.
o If you are a member of a religious group:
  o Share your plan with members of your church group in whom you have trust and confidence.
  o Add your plan to a prayer-group or a study group for support and encouragement.
  o Harness the emotional component of Scripture passages that promote growth to maturity in Christ.
o Share your success with family and friends.
o Lead a group discussion (in person or online) on how you have accomplished your changes. Share details about your life that illustrate growth you are comfortable for others to know.
o If you want to become a coach and get paid for helping other people to make life changes, start constructing a plan of how you will establish your qualifications.

I got started in coaching by connecting with active coaches. The first coach training I enrolled in was based on the principles established by Sir John Whitmore in his book *Coaching for Performance: The Principles and Practice of Coaching and Leadership.*[6] This is an easy self-study primer. The fifth edition of this book was published in 2017, shortly after Sir John died.

> THINK ABOUT THE POSITIVE QUALITIES OF THE WARRIOR, THE MIRACLE-WORKER, THE LOVER, AND THE RULER.

After setting this foundation, which you can do on your own, connect with a program that gets you certified as a coach in the specialty you choose. The GROW model, as explained in Whitmore's book, is a good foundation for coaching. There are no minimum educational requirements to become a certified coach.

If you do the recommended actions above, I guarantee that it will make a difference in your life, in your love, your wellness, and happiness.

For one final contemplative exercise, look at the diagram below. Think about the four loves, the four dimensions of function, the four archetypes. Think about the positive qualities of the Warrior, the Miracle-Worker, the Lover, and the Ruler. If you are a Christian, think about growing into maturity in Christ. If you are not a Christian, connect with your deepest beliefs about a purpose in life. Think about what qualities you want to see more of in your life. Compose a short prayer or affirmation that may drive your action plan.

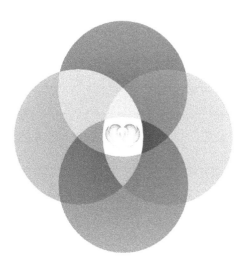

NOTES FOR YOUR BOOK

_____

_____

_____

_____

Please use these lines to start composing your OPUS and list other items of your action plan.

_____

_____

_____

_____

_____

_____

_____

_____

_____

_____

_____

_____

_____

APPENDICES

APPENDIX I

MENTAL AND PSYCHOLOGICAL SKILLS FOR STRESS REDUCTION, STRESS MANAGEMENT, AND INCREASING HAPPINESS

The data and personal testimonies about these skills and protocols support they are effective. It is a matter of practice and consistency. When these fit with the spiritual foundation, they assist in wellness promotion, spiritual uplift, increased happiness, and life enjoyment. My purpose here is to give an introduction to each one and provide an authoritative reference. I have arranged them in alphabetical order.

o **Deep breathing**
This is sometimes called Diaphragmatic Breathing. Most of us get by with shallow breathing, using the ribcage to move air. Deep breathing calls for actively involving the diaphragm and is recommended as short breaks while having to sit for a long time. The steps are:

   o   Sit upright, with feet firmly on the floor.
   o   Inhale deeply so the abdomen gets raised.

- o Completely exhale while tightening the abdominal muscles.
- o Caution: do only two or three deep breaths in a row as more may trigger hyperventilation and dizziness. (As my wife's brother, Harold Grosboll, read this he mentioned falling and having to get stitches on his forehead because he did too many deep breaths in a row.)
- o Benefits: gets extra oxygen to the body and especially the brain. This can energize and fend off drowsiness at work.
- o Reference: https://www.health.harvard.edu/mind-and-mood/relaxation-techniques-breath-control-helps-quell-errant-stress-response

- o **Flow**
  The research psychologist Mihaly Csikszentmihalyi (pronounced "mee-high cheek-sent-mee-high) was the first to describe the state of flow—a state of heightened focus while being productive and enjoying it. His first book on the subject, *Flow: The Psychology of Optimal Experience* was published in 1990. In February 2004, he presented a TED Talk, available on YouTube, which gives a 20-minute overview of his research. It includes seven descriptors of the state of flow:

- o Complete focus on what you are doing
- o Feeling a sense of ecstasy
- o A clear sense of what needs to be done and how well you are doing it
- o Knowing the task is doable and you have the skills to do it
- o A sense of serenity
- o Loss of the awareness of time

   ○   Getting the task accomplished as its own reward

This video, "Flow, the secret to happiness" has been very popular in wellness lectures.
Reference: https://www.ted.com/talks/mihaly_csikszentmihalyi_flow_the_secret_to_happiness#t-4721

○ **Forgiving**
Forgiving someone who has either hurt or wronged you, or asking forgiveness of someone you have hurt or wronged goes a long way in healing the mind. It gets rid of tangled circuits that code regrets and desire for revenge. Combined with spiritual rituals it is a powerful act of healing for both parties.

   ○   This requires communication through letter-writing, text messaging, email, or a phone call.
   ○   Ask for permission to broach the topic, or use the least confrontational method to start the conversation.
   ○   If religious, pray about the matter before taking any steps.
   ○   Caution: different people are at different stages of readiness to heal. Be sure to start the communication in a calm, non-accusatory tone, and plan ahead to avoid angry outbursts.
   ○   Reminder, forgiving yourself is part of this process.
   ○   Reference: https://greatergood.berkeley.edu/article/item/eight_keys_to_forgiveness

○ **Gratitude**
Psychologists debate whether gratitude is a trait, a mood, or an emotion. I think the attitude and practice of being thankful, grateful, and appreciative is a mix of all three. Our upbringing programs how we express ourselves, helps

us acknowledge how we value help from others, and how we appreciate what we have.

Practicing gratitude goes beyond the everyday "Thank you" and "You're welcome." It goes beyond acknowledging gifts with thank you cards. To tap the deeper feelings of gratitude, researchers recommend actions such as:

o Keeping a gratitude journal by writing down each day three things for which you are thankful. Or, write three things that went well for the day or week, and why.
o Counting your blessings—write down or tell someone up to five things that were blessings each week.
o Write about what life might be like if certain good things did not happen.
o Write a gratitude letter or make a gratitude visit to someone who significantly impacted your life, and you have not told them about it in a while.
o Reference: https://ggsc.berkeley.edu/ search?q=gratitude

o **Intentional acts of kindness**
Kindness starts with you—be kind to yourself. It is unrealistic to respond to every human need that comes to our attention. Among all the opportunities to do acts of kindness for others, those that seem to generate the greatest positive health effects include:

o Meeting a need with no concern for a reward
o Allowing yourself to experience the feelings of compassion, which precede the act of kindness

○ Adding an item into the budget to support random acts of kindness, such as paying for lunch or gas for someone in line behind you

○ References: https://www.health.harvard.edu/blog/the-heart-and-science-of-kindness-2019041816447

Script for a lovingkindness meditation: https://ggia.berkeley.edu/practice/loving_kindness_meditation. Research shows intentional acts of kindness release the hormones oxytocin (the love hormone) and dopamine (the pleasure hormone).

○ **Laughter—A Sense of Humor**

○ "Laughter is the best medicine" is a very popular statement. The health effects of laughter are well established and many institutions incorporate it in treating patients. That began with the experience of Norman Cousins as told in his book *Anatomy of an Illness as Perceived by the Patient* (1979). In his experience, laughter was a better pain reliever and sleep inducer than morphine.

○ Another early example of how humor can promote health is the story of Patch Adams and the Gesundheit! Institute (https://www.patchadams.org/patch-adams/).

○ Both stories above have been popularized in movies. As of this writing (2021), Patch Adams is still alive and carries on his work in Urbana, Illinois.

○ Laughter and a good sense of humor have been shown to increase the hormones that generate good feelings (dopamine, serotonin, endorphins), decrease the stress hormones cortisol and epinephrine, and boost the immune system. One fairly recent review of the research was published in the journal *Advances in*

Physiology Education (Vol 41, # 3) in a paper titled "Humor, Laughter, Learning, and Health: A Brief Review" by Brandon M. Savage, *et al.*

- **Massage**
  The health benefits of massage therapy are well established.

    - If your health insurance covers part of the fee for massage therapy, it is worth it—it is even worth the expense without insurance.
    - Learning to do massages for a love partner is a worthwhile skill.
    - Gentle, feather-like massages for children are very relaxing and sleep inducing. (Our kids gave it the name "the specialty.")
    - References: https://www.mayoclinic.org/healthy-lifestyle/stress-management/in-depth/massage/art-20045743

- **Meditation**
  It took a while before I fully embraced the practice and benefits of meditation. Something in my religious upbringing had coded a caution about possible mind-control practices, especially when *transcendental* was a popular word in meditation vocabulary. I've come to experience the calming effects of meditation and find no conflicts with my Christian beliefs.

  Different forms of meditation may have different benefits. Those who research such things have made excellent summaries available for the public. What I recommend to my students is to survey the methods available to see how they fit with your core beliefs. Then, invest the time to practice building a habit. I use the relaxation response and a personal composite of methods I call "Practicing God's Presence." The types of meditation studied and recommended by psychologists and researchers for their health benefits include:

- o Spiritual Meditation and Presence—quiet contemplation triggered by a passage of scripture or a prayer.
- o Mindfulness Meditation and Practice—to develop the habit of being fully aware of the present moment while calmly accepting whatever feelings, body sensations, or thoughts existing at the moment. The Harvard University reference below gives a summary of benefits, and the step-by-step practice.
- o The Relaxation Response—this is a very practical, research-established process to bring calm and reduced tension to your whole body. You say a focus word in concert with your breathing. My focus word is "peace." The step-by-step protocol is given by Dr. Benson himself in the third reference below. (I believe the Benson/Henry Institute at Mass General Hospital will keep this video up even after Dr. Benson is gone.)
- o Training in structured meditation can aim to influence feelings, presence, and perspective. The social-emotional protocol of "loving-kindness meditation" has been shown to increase attention and compassion.
- o References:
  - https://www.helpguide.org/harvard/benefits-of-mindfulness.htm
  - https://mindworks.org/blog/different-types-meditation-technique/
  - https://bensonhenryinstitute.org/about-us-dr-herbert-benson/
  - https://greatergood.berkeley.edu/article/item/what_type_of_meditation_is_best_for_you

o **Namaste**
In this period of socially distanced greetings, I have picked up the practice of using "Namaste" (nuh-MUH-stay). It feels extra special because of my Indian heritage. I use it with the meaning of a greeting.

- o I bow to honor the other person as an equal or better, especially if older.
- o I do not use it for any spiritual, theological purpose or belief.
- o Reference (not research-based, just knowledge-based): https://www.gaia.com/article/meaning-of-namaste

o **Progressive muscle relaxation**
This is simply a mental scan of body tension followed by letting go of tightness and tension beginning with the toes and ending on the skull. Users of meditation and relaxation techniques use this to prepare for the meditation or relaxation procedure.

- o The process is to tense then slowly relax one muscle group at a time.
- o Reference: https://www.mayoclinic.org/ healthy-lifestyle/stress-management/in-depth/ relaxation-technique/art-20045368

o **Rehearsing**
We are all accustomed to practice and rehearsal in preparation for an event or production. You go through all the steps of the production, then do a "dress rehearsal" to simulate the real event.

The rehearsal we are talking about here involves practice, but it is more a mental activity—to go through the process in your mind. This calls for the use of visualization (doing the act in your mind), and imagery (seeing yourself go through the motion). This is used a lot in athletic training. Benefits of this process that combine rehearsal with visualization and imagery include:

o It helps to manage emotions and increase confidence.
o It reduces anxiety and improves concentration
o Reference: https://www.bbc.co.uk/bitesize/guides/zgntfrd/revision/1
o https://www.psychologytoday.com/us/blog/living-forward/201806/3-effective-visualization-techniques-change-your-life

o **Savoring**
This is one of the hot topics in positive psychology. It means taking time to focus on good things and the enjoyment they bring to your consciousness. The attention (mindfulness) focused on good, pleasurable experiences enhances the emotional reward. The advice is to:

o Savor the past. Relive pleasant memories and explore them for details you may have overlooked before. You may even imagine what you might have done to make the experience even better.
o Savor the present. As positive things happen, pay attention to the emotions, the cause/effective relationships, and the desire to have more of the same.
o Capitalize on the positive events: Tell it. Show it. Share it. (Not in a boastful, prideful way but in a genuine "wish you were there with me" way if appropriate.)
o Savor the future. Anticipate good things from your plans and goals. Use your imagination to anticipate positive experiences.

- o References: https://www.psychologytoday.
  com/us/blog/click-here-happiness/201807/
  what-is-savoring-and-why-is-it-the-key-happiness
- o https://greatergood.berkeley.edu/article/item/10_
  steps_to_savoring_the_good_things_in_life

The above stress management skills have been shown by many researchers to promote health and happiness. One mechanism of this effect is via brain chemicals. There are four chemicals that are being termed the "happy hormones." These are: dopamine (generate good feelings), serotonin (stabilize mood), endorphins (pain killers) and oxytocin (promote love and bonding). A reliable, credible summary of these effects are given in the Harvard University 2019 publication titled: "Positive Psychology: Harnessing the power of happiness, mindfulness and inner strength" (https://www.health.harvard. edu/special-health-reports/positive-psychology-harnessing-the-power-of-happiness-mindfulness-and-inner-strength?utm_source=HHPBlog&utm_medium=link&utm_content=related-text&utm_campaign=referral).

APPENDIX 2
EMOTIONAL HIGHS AND LOWS

My hot temper

This was the source of most of my regrets in life. The most vivid memory of my uncontrolled anger is the picture in my head with a butcher knife raised, ready to plunge it into the back of one of my brothers during an all-out fight. Fortunately, another brother was close by and reached us in time to grab my hand before it came down. I shudder to think of the consequences of that incident had it not been stopped. I know I used to lose touch with reality when in a fit of rage. Sometimes, I wonder about a definition of demon possession.

For the last 35 years, I don't think I have lost control of that temper even once. It is not something I have to exert effort to accomplish—it just died over time with some mindfulness effort, life experiences, and the grace of God. Now, I see one quality of water in this. I can absorb a lot of heat without getting hot! And I savor that!

Acting

At 17 years of age, I was chosen to play St. Paul in a production of the play "The Life of Paul." I still enjoy the euphoria I felt at the end of the concert, having flawlessly delivered St. Paul's speeches and passion to a full concert hall. (I felt ready for Hollywood!)

Our first son's birth

I didn't expect to be in the labor room with her, but the doctor asked my wife if she thought I could handle being there and called me in. I stood close to the table, gently cradling her head with both hands. Suddenly, the doctor dropped the scalpel in time to catch the little guy as he seemed in a hurry to break free. In the excitement, I had squeezed so hard on my wife's head she ended up with a headache and imprints of my thumbs on her forehead.

Singing in a production of "Handel's Messiah."

(I write this also as a tribute in loving memory of our choir director, Marianne Scriven.) Oh, the heights of spiritual joy when a 40-voice choir and full orchestra put in the work to practice, and render *Messiah* to a full concert hall. I was in the second tenor section (my wife was in the first soprano section), not because I had a great singing voice, but just because I loved to sing and that is what the choir director encouraged.

The joy of dancing

I grew up strongly indoctrinated that dancing was a sin. I carefully avoided any dancing until I saw how much fun Uncle Toby was having as he danced at a niece's wedding. I joined him and several cousins and had a ball. I figured that the objection to dancing was based on the potential for simulating sexual movements. If you move and jump around more like calisthenics, make wild arms and head motions while keeping the hips balanced over the legs, you can have a lot of fun. Just show that you feel the rhythm of the music. Nowadays, I join in any dancing at weddings or other social occasions. And I take prideful pleasure in seeing a granddaughter become a professional ballet dancer.

The pleasure of playing Pickleball

I was a racquetball player for 32 years. For my sixty-eight birthday, I decided to explore a new activity and found Pickleball listed on the Parks & Rec offerings in Martinsburg, West Virginia. I enrolled and found the new sport to be very engaging, easy to learn, and less demanding on the aging body. My first coaches were Patty, Diane & Randy, Judy, Reine & Arley, and Donna. I invited my neighbor to join, and Mark became one of the best players. The activity is perfect for indoors or outdoors, gives a moderate aerobic workout, and is suitable for all ages. The social interactions and friendships that develop are truly ongoing blessings. For my 70th birthday, the Pickleball group generously supported my project to raise $3,000 to purchase a used car for one of my students who was pregnant with twins. I continue to create memories with this group and make new friends through this rapidly spreading sport. I take my paddle wherever I travel.

Being part of a loving neighborhood
In our 50 years of marriage, we have moved about 25 times and lived in six different states in the USA. Our retirement home in West Virginia has proved to be the best neighborhood in which we have lived. The close neighborhood is a group of twelve homes on a cul-de-sac. Here are three examples of the kindnesses and friendship that developed in this group of three retired couples and nine families with young children.

One winter morning at breakfast time, I got a call from the Indian couple across the street: "Check on your front porch." There was a huge bowl of hot sambar, accompanied by idlis from Raja and Sarada. On a recent occasion, we had a snowstorm. I had stayed in the hospital with my wife who had major surgery the day before. We got a message from Kevin: "Don't worry about it, your driveway will be cleared by the time you get home." One of my joys in spring and summer is to ride a tractor to mow the lawn. But I don't own this riding mower. Mark owns the tractor, and keeps it in my garage, Kevin pays for the gas, and I get to ride and cut two or sometimes three lawns. And two of the lawns have hilly sections that offer some challenge to driving. In winter,

Kevin uses his snow-blower on all three driveways. I don't want to move from this neighborhood.

The most embarrassing incident of my life

When I was a teenager, there was a clear division of what was "boys' work," and what was "girls' work." Boys would go to the fields and tend the animals or crops. Girls would cook and do the laundry. At this point in our family's life, there were no girls to do the laundry. It was also the time when doing laundry meant you had to put a basket of dirty clothes on your head, walk to the river half-mile away, and launder clothes on the river stones. I will never forget the day I walked that half-mile with a basket of clothes including dirty diapers. I set up on a river stone to start the laundry as the only male among a dozen women and girls. Memorable redemption: two of the girls pitied me. They came over and took care of my basket of clothes while I sat on the riverbank and watched them.

My fears about "perilous times"

I grew up in a church which was very deep into prophecies about the end-times, and the disasters that will occur as we approach the end of the world. As a teenager, I was fearful about things like: "the time of trouble," or "the close of probation," and "the seven last plagues." At one time, I felt I could explain all the imagery and predictions of the book of Daniel in the Old Testament, and the book of Revelation in the New Testament. I have not paid much attention to all those topics and the beliefs I had about them in over 40 years.

It seems that my church doesn't preach much on these topics anymore. And I'm not fearful anymore. The week after the mob invasion of the Capitol in Washington, DC, I had the task of presenting a devotional at a Zoom meeting. The thoughts that came to mind were to start with the scripture about "perilous times" in 2 Timothy 3. Verses 1–7 and describe the behaviors of men that precipitate perilous times. (I pointed out to the group that this was an indictment of men only, women seemed to be exempted.) Then I reviewed chapter 13 of the book of Revelation in which the roles played by a dragon, a leopard that has the feet of a bear and the mouth of a lion, and a lamb with two horns which spoke like a dragon. I used to know what all these symbolisms meant. Now, I don't.

Somewhere in there, I remember something about the United States getting to a point where constitutional rule is overthrown. I never could conceive of that happening—until January 6, 2021. So, I raised the question in my group about the need and the usefulness to review what we used to believe about perilous times and end-times. I think we will schedule a series of Zoom discussions around these topics. (A free copy of the book *The Great Controversy Between Christ and Satan* is available from Project Gutenberg at http://www.gutenberg.org/ebooks/25833. This book greatly influenced my understanding of end-times, and will be part of the projected review.)

Sitting in the hospital waiting room while my wife was near death
She was bleeding out as fast as the blood transfusions went in. Compounding the physical trauma was the emotional trauma of the loss of our second child at four months into the pregnancy. When her blood pressure got to 60 over 40, a nurse came out to tell me to expect the worst. I recall thinking about life without her. Our first born was only nine months old. My wife pulled out of it and later she said, "I kept fighting to get back to you and Mike."

At my dying mother's bedside
During the early morning hours of the day she died, I was alone in the hospital room with her. Her favorite album of songs by Jim Reeves was in the CD player. I sat close to her right ear and sang

along: "Across the Bridge," "Precious Memories," "Oh, Gentle Shepherd," "This World is Not My Home," and "Take My Hand, Precious Lord." She squeezed my hand—my final goodbye. She was pronounced dead four hours later surrounded by our Dad and the whole family with one member on the phone.

My tribute at my mother's funeral service
I told a few stories about her. One was when she snatched one of the younger children from drowning in a swim-hole at the river when she couldn't swim. Another was about her casual statement "I knew you would come," when I showed up at her door in St. Croix after Hurricane Hugo. A third was about her chiding me on a visit after a very long absence, "Where have you been for so long?" I recall the ending to that tribute:

> *I can just see her now at the resurrection. She'll turn to her angel and say, "Any old crown will do." Then, she'll push her way to the head of the line to meet her Lord. She'll look into His wonderful face and say, "Where have you been for so long?" Then rather quickly, "I knew you'd come."*

> *And the King of Kings would say softly and tenderly, "Well done, you good and faithful servant. Enter into the joys."*

> *Sleep, dear mother. You deserve to rest from your labors. Sleep, loving grandmother, your angel awaits to usher you into your Lord's presence at the resurrection. Sleep, precious great-grandmother, sleep, and your works will follow you. We'll see you in the morning.*

The joys of seeing grandchildren achieve substantive goals
Carol and I take deep, humble pride in seeing our grandchildren achieve their goals. Our oldest, Kaitlyn, earned a full scholarship including board and books to Western Kentucky University. She graduated in 2018, *Magna Cum Laude*, with a major in biology.

It was with great pride that I listened to her name announced at her graduation. She got married under PN-20 conditions, and we look forward to a great grand-child. It is a pleasure to accept her help in critiquing my writing and giving the insights of a mid-twentysomething on love, wellness, and happiness. I'm especially proud that she was a biology major. She outperformed me—I never got close to *cum laude*.

Our second, Lauren, is a freshman at the University of Virginia, a professional ballet dancer, and in the process of filling her portfolio for modeling jobs on the side.

Our third, William, is going on 17 years of age, has a captain's certification in sailing, and completed his solo flight towards his pilot's license on February 21, 2021.

Our fourth is the miracle baby. Born as a micro-preemie weighing in at one pound nine ounces, he is all caught up physically and developmentally as he approaches his fifth birthday.

We look forward to celebrating future achievements and success. However, our most important emotional gift to them is to let them know that we love and value them for who they are, and nothing bad or good that happens can make us love them any less or more.

(Oh, guys, the Christmas 2021 sail from Grenada to St. Vincent is booked!)

****

Emotions are the fuel that fire up the engines of the human spirit to act. The early disciples of Christ had the emotional charge needed. They had confidence in the stickiest of messages ("He is risen!"). The context of conflicts under Roman rulership provided the opportunities to reach and change their world.

Current disciples of Christ have the right context and opportunities to reach and change the world. The challenge is to demonstrate "He is risen" by growing to maturity in Christ.

And the right people are coming together in small groups to fuel a surge of love, wellness, and happiness. You are never so happy as when you have loved long and well, and get to expend yourself in work you truly enjoy.

APPENDIX 3
MY BEST SERMON?

During my late teens, and up to 21 years of age, my most enjoyable mental activity was to compose and deliver sermons as a lay preacher in our church. After I started college in a science curriculum, that joy was absent from my life. Later in life, I had a few opportunities to preach, but most of the churches I attended had full-time preachers. As I look back, I recall three of my sermons.

The first was titled "The Form of the Fourth." I was 20 years old and the story of three Hebrew boys surviving the "burning fiery furnace," which was made seven times hotter than usual, fascinated me. I had some thoughts to share about what people see when they look into the furnaces in our lives. Do they see "The Form of the Fourth?"

The second sermon was titled "The Jonah Syndrome." As a biology professor at a religious college, I was invited to preach at a service organized by an association of South Asians. I shared my reflections on running away from "a calling," based on the story of Jonah and the whale.

I wrote my third sermon "C is for What Matters Most" in response to a sermon competition. That script came together in a timeframe of about two hours after attending an all-day event at the Willow Creek Community Church in Chicago, Illinois.

The sermon competition was on the theme of a health education model using CELEBRATIONS as an acronym for important aspects of health and well-being. I had read the announcement and decided to enter the competition. The following weekend, a group of us left Maryland and drove to Chicago to attend the convention at Willow.

The C in CELEBRATIONS had already been assigned for "Choice," a key determinant of health. After participating in the all-day program of songs and sermons on Christ at Willow, I was inspired to write a sermon suggesting the C in CELEBRATIONS should be for Christ.

The sermon won the competition. *Ministry Magazine*, was supposed to publish it but didn't. I accepted the cash prize but felt really disappointed the sermon was not published Was it my pride? I think I have gotten over that, but I wanted to preserve and share that sermon. It is the only one of the three for which I have a copy. So here it is, published in my book for sharing and preservation, exactly as it was submitted, typos and all.

"C" IS FOR WHAT MATTERS MOST

Many of you can recall the times in your church or school programs when you had a part in an acrostic. You and your fellow classmates spelled out a word or phrase one letter at a time. You memorized your part. You proudly held up the letter that was yours and you said it as best you could. A short, powerful statement for you and your audience to remember. A compact message about something important to life and eternity.

Today, I want to reflect on the word CELEBRATIONS, the word that captures our General Conference Health Ministries Department's vision for health promotion in this new century. The acrostic, in its shortest form is:

C is for Choice,
E is for Exercise,
L is for Liquids,
E is for Environment,
B is for Belief,
R is for Rest,
A is for Air,
T is for Temperance,
I is for Integrity,
O is for Optimism,
N is for Nutrition, and
S is for Social Support

I want to focus on the first letter of this word in a few thoughts titled " 'C' Is for What Matters Most."

"What matters most" is the new catch phrase of the philosophy that is leading twenty-first century business thinking. "What matters most" is the primary question that is used in the coaching paradigm. And coaching as a new profession is growing by the proverbial leaps and bounds. "What matters most," as well as "acting on what matters most," is at the heart of Peter Block's book, *The Answer to How is Yes.*

"What matters most" is the core of two questions asked by Jesus to his disciples in Matthew chapter 16 beginning with verse 13. "When Jesus came to Caesarea Phillipi, he asked his disciples, 'Who are the people saying I am?' Verse 14: "Well," they replied, "some say John the Baptist; some, Elijah; some, Jeremiah or one of the prophets."

But that was only a part of what mattered most. Jesus brought the question home to the heart of each disciple. Verse 15: Then he asked them, "Who do you think I am?" These two questions of Jesus point to one major fact of His ministry: What mattered most was whether the real purpose of His mission was getting through to us.

One brash, impetuous disciple knew only one way to express what he thought – upfront, clear and succinct. Verse 16 of Matthew chapter 16: "Simon Peter answered, 'The Christ, the Messiah, the Son of the living God.'"

My point is that what matters most is Christ. And my proposal is that the "C" in CELEBRATIONS should boldly proclaim that "C" is for Christ.

Now, before the brethren think I am critical of the scholars who spent many hours of hard work to create the wording for each letter in CELEBRATIONS, let me hasten to say that I agree that "C is for Choices" is a very good piece of the model. I see a carefully worded definition of the importance that choices play in our health and well-being. Such clarity in definitions comes after much longer descriptions are circulated, and a wording that is clear and focused is selected. This is a great thought to begin any consideration of action for health promotion. Let me quote the full statement:

"C is for choices—the cradle of your destiny. You may not always see the end from the beginning, but your choices always determine your destiny. Healthy choices bring positive effects to the individual, family, and community. Unhealthy choices drain vitality from the entire populace. No person is an island. Celebrate your freedom to make healthy choices – it is the tool that opens all the other good gifts of health."

As the first letter of the word CELEBRATIONS, the letter "C" and its definition in the acrostic have great impact. Impact by position and clarity of message. So my question is: did we miss an opportunity to impact the world of health promotion with an upfront, clear message about the "C" at the forefront of all true health and healing? The "C" behind real well-being in the here and now, and the hereafter?

So I say to you today, "C" is for Christ, and that is what matters most to Christians all over the world. That is what matters most to our reason for being in this world. That is what matters most to God's work of reconciling the world to Himself and promoting health for all on earth, and perfect health for eternity.

In this postmodern era, we have become so careful to be politically correct, to be scientifically sound, and not to affront anyone's belief system, that we find ways to present our beliefs in carefully crafted, palatable platitudes. Crafting general statements that conform to secular science is a great strategy when we write for the secular world, or when we prepare materials to be used in secular schools or government agencies.

But when we prepare materials for ourselves, and for other Christians, why not take the risk and be bold and brash. Why don't we really express what matters most and help each other to act on what matters most?

I imagine that on the committee that prepared the CELEBRATIONS definitions, at least one member must have suggested that the "C" should stand for Christ. I imagine that the discussion went like this:

Proponent of C is for Christ: "My fellow committee members, I see here a wonderful opportunity to focus our health promotion efforts on Christ. He has promised that if we lift Him up, He will draw the people to him. He is the answer to the transformation of lifestyle that we are seeking to promote among us. As we lift Him up through the power of the Holy Spirit, we will see the results in changed lives. And we will accumulate more than enough statistical data to show that this is the best way to optimum health and well-being."

Proponent of C is for Choice: "My fellow committee members, I believe in what our good member here proposes. Yes, Christ is the answer to life transformation. But if we are too simplistic in our message, we may be regarded as naïve. We are a church that has done the studies and substantiated major claims of our health message through the scientific method. If we lead off with an unscientific statement like "Christ is the answer to health promotion," we will not be taken seriously. And our colleagues in the health promotion field may lose respect for our scholarship. Besides, if we show that we understand the current scientific literature on cognitive skills and behavioral change, we can bring Christ in later. After we engage people in dialogue about the power of choice to bring about change, we can lead them into dialogue about the power of Christ. And then, we can recommend that one option is to choose Christ."

Suddenly, from the back of this imaginary meeting room, a stranger in fisherman's clothes slowly gets to his feet. His presence commands rapt attention.

Simon Peter: "My fellow committee members, I understand your dilemma. In this postmodern era, it is difficult to be simple, and risky to appear naïve. But I say, go with the simple. Lead off with a bold statement that Christ is the answer to lifestyle transformation, and then talk about choice and other scientific knowledge of behavioral strategies for change. I guarantee you that you'll see such dramatic results in peoples' lives, that the data will accumulate and surprise the scientific community. And while you are thinking about what other dialogue to engage people in, think about these: 'C' is for Crucified; 'C' is for Coming again. What a celebration that will be! And, my fellow witnesses, we just can't leave out this one: 'C' is for Comforter."

It is difficult to find one's true voice among the multitude of health promotion proponents on the scene today. It is not difficult to draw our focus back to the simple message that all personal transformation in the lives of Christians is founded on belief in Christ. Unless, of course, we really believe that the science of exercising choice is the primary foundation, and choosing Christ is secondary. We didn't choose Him. He first loved and chose us.

The other side of the argument to lead with "C is for Christ" is that by leading with a statement proclaiming our belief in Christ we may turn away people who have interests in health and in our church. This is a valid point. In being "wise as serpents and harmless as doves," we want to word our messages so that we don't turn people off with naïve, unscientific claims.

I wonder if by leading with "C is for Choice," instead of "C is for Christ," we are not putting more importance on the human element for change rather than on the divine. Of course, to focus on the human element is all that the scientific method can do. I wonder if, to summarize a few thoughts from Peter Block, we are not "catering to the popular culture by surrendering what matters most for what works." 22

We have a most powerful method of health promotion and we are not using it nor sharing it with the boldness, enthusiasm, and inspiration it deserves. How do we move to a higher level of action to demonstrate the health promoting effects of a Christ-centered life? The answer may be another question: how do we build a culture that expresses what matters most? The answer to this "how" is a "yes" to Christ. And that leads to a "what" question.

What does it look like to live the culture of Christ? Four characteristics of Christ can be translated into practical cultural values to lead health and wellness promotion:

- o *He is Warrior.* "Then there was war in heaven. Michael and the angels under His command fought the dragon and his angels." Rev 12: 7. Christ (Michael) was the first warrior. A warrior culture for soldiers in His army calls for physical fitness and self-discipline.
- o *He is Miracle-Worker.* Christ's work on earth was characterized by miracles and great transformations in the lives He touched. Christians are called to work for transformation of lives through known processes and principles, and through the miraculous. "The truth is, anyone who believes in me will do the same works I have done, and even greater works…" John 14:12. A miracle-worker culture calls us to act with faith and prayer and confidence in the humanly impossible.
- o *He is Lover.* God first loved and gave His Son, who loved and gave His life. (John 3:16, Galatians 2: 20) A love culture removes all barriers that maintain inequalities. A love culture brings harmony and value to one another. It is the only place where racial and national and ethnic differences that now cause so much unhealthiness can be healed. It is the only process of real healing for broken relationships.
- o *He is King.* "On his robe and thigh was written this title: King of kings and Lord of lords." Rev 19:16. If Christ is King then his followers are royalty. A culture

of royalty is characterized by graciousness, and kindness, and compassion and responsibility for the kingdom and its other subjects. It is also marked by our attempt to do whatever we do with the highest quality.

The culture of Christ is characterized by being and living positive values, instead of focusing on factors about deficits, disease, and death. Positivity, virtues and action are the language of the new profession of coaching.

Coaching has brought a paradigm shift to health education. In coaching, a coach and a coachee engage in conversations that begin with what matters most to the coachee, not to the coach. Transformations are promoted not by information, but by what the coachee decides are the important actions to take.

In the issue of *Ministry* magazine that carried the invitation to submit sermons on the CELEBRATIONS theme, there is an article by James Cress titled "Lifting up Jesus." I think this article provides a nice balance between presenting Christ and presenting our scholarship. Before introducing the book, *The Essential Jesus*, and the strong scholarship that contributed to its compilation, Cress presented Jesus in these words:

"Adventists, of all people, should emphasize Jesus more and more as the author and finisher of Christian faith. Jesus' eternal, perpetual existence, creative power, communicative initiative toward humanity, miraculous birth, exemplary life, compassionate ministry, substitutionary death at Calvary, victorious resurrection and ascension, priestly ministry on our behalf in heavenly places, plus His promised soon return, must be the recurring theme and most prominent feature of all our proclamation if we are to fulfill the mission of lifting up Jesus before our world." [33]

Can we dare to lift up Jesus in our health promotion materials? Are we ready to proclaim "C is for Christ" and take the consequences, reap the rewards, and celebrate the results?

If we believe that Christ is the primary solution to all human woes; if we believe that Christ is the answer to our postmodern spiritual hunger; if we truly believe that dramatic improvements in lifestyle can be triggered through the empowering cleansing of an in-dwelling Christ; then let us boldly proclaim that the "C" in CELEBRATIONS is for Christ. "C" is for what matters most.

"And when I am lifted up, I will draw everyone to me" (John 12:32). Let us go forth and lift up a risen, ascended, and soon coming Savior in our personal health promotion plans.

It's high time to act on what matters most.

REFERENCES:

[1] *Ministry*, March 2002, p.24
[2] Block, Peter. *The Answer to How is Yes.* Berrett-Koehler Publishers, Inc., San Francisco, 2002, pp. 1, 4 & 79.
[3] *Ministry*, March 2002, p. 27

APPENDIX 4
LESSONS FROM OUR INTER-RACIAL MARRIAGE

Carol and I met in 1969 and got married in 1970. We received the following advice and objections from very good people on both sides:

o "You have only known each other for less than a year. This is all romantic passion and your marriage will only last a year."

o "Your children will suffer in this skin-color-conscious society."

o "Indian men are too sexually demanding. A white woman may have a rough time in the sex-life of such a marriage."

o "How can you even tolerate standing beside a colored man, much more being in bed with one?"

o "Don't let them do it. They will not be able to travel in the deep south."

o "The sociology of race relations is like this: only lower class, low self-esteem white women marry men of non-white races."

o "Get what you can, then ditch her. She's only white-trash, anyway."

As part of our life review for our 50th wedding anniversary, we reflected on how things turned out. We saw how the social changes over the last 50 years made life less complicated for inter-racial couples. We wish all those who predicted failure and misery were alive to see how things turned out for us. Those who are alive may have forgotten their opinions and advice.

In *Love, Wellness, and Happiness,* we have encouraged readers to examine their lives, beliefs, goals, and values, and act on their understanding. Our reflections included the following:

- o Generalizations about sexual differences among races are not the best criteria on which to base decisions about marriage. Most people have opinions and beliefs inherited from their culture and experience. One anecdote about an Indian man chasing his wife around the house daily is insufficient to predict what a couple's sexual compatibility may be.
- o Our children did not experience any name-calling, bullying, or social devaluation because of their biracial heritage. In fact, they received many compliments on their complexion and physique, even from babyhood. Maybe, we were fortunate that life kept us mostly within communities that were more integrated and liberal. It is intriguing that we now have a granddaughter who fits perfectly within the professions of ballet dancing and modeling. It seems like the Indian-Irish-Italian genetic mix has produced a masterpiece. We look forward to seeing the blend of positive qualities that shine through great physical beauty. She's already a disciplined, hardworking warrior.
- o Some people grow up with a strong aversion to darker skin pigmentation. Finding it unpleasant to even stand beside a human of different skin color may call for some self-examination. Carol's experience in high school choir

reminds us of that. She was asked to change places with one girl who couldn't endure standing beside a black boy. A person with that aversion should not decide for a person without it.

o Traveling in the deep south was not a very high priority goal as we contemplated marriage. We laughed about that advice when we got lost in Alabama on a road-trip in 2017. Maybe, all the dangers had passed by our 47th anniversary.

o Social class and educational status do play roles in marriage in general and inter-racial marriages in particular. A recent study titled "Marrying Up by Marrying Down: Status Exchange between Social Origin and Education in the United States" (https://www.ncbi.nlm.nih.gov/pmc/articles/PMC5214284/) explored some of those factors. In our case, we were pursuing higher education and carving out our social status together.

o One-fifth of the way through the 21st century is a good time to make the effort to discard all the derogatory terms we have used to put down other individuals and races.

What factors contribute to the success or failure of a marriage? In 1986, Drs. John Gottman and Robert Levenson established the "Love Lab" at the University of Washington. They studied newly-weds by observing how the couples interact and communicate while solving conflicts. They combined physiologic data with behavior and personality traits. From their data analyses, they could predict which couples would remain married (the masters), and which couples would divorce within six years (the disasters). They calculated that when there are at least five times more positive than negative interactions between partners, their marriage would last. Positive interactions included kindness, generosity, affection, humor, interest in the other person, excitement, empathy, gentleness, and optimism.

Negative interaction included hostility, disappointment, anger, pessimism, harshness, distrust, criticism, defensiveness, contempt, stonewalling, and denigration. Very valuable insights on lasting relationships are available from

- o The Gottman Institute, run by Dr. Gottman and his wife, fellow researcher/therapist Dr. Julie Schwartz Gottman (https://www.gottman.com/about/research/)
- o Dr. Gottman's book *What Makes Love Last? How to build trust and avoid betrayal—Secrets from the Love Lab* (Simon & Schuster, 2012)
- o "The Science of Love" TED Talk, Oct 2018 (https://www.ted.com/talks/john_gottman_the_science_of_love/transcript?language=en)

I think Carol and I have had a ratio of ten to one regarding our positive to negative reactions to conflicts and disagreements. We have been lucky with strong compatibility on the four levels of love: eros, storge, philia, and agape. We produced three good children. We have been creative partners for intellectual products. She has been my alpha reader for everything I have written since we met. We have had positive regard for each other irrespective of physical state and health status. We faced setbacks as challenges to overcome together. It was, "you and me against the world of naysayers." We both shared the belief in God's love and guidance.

I do hope our story will be an encouragement to you on your journey. We all deal with inter-racial challenges in one form or another as citizens of one world.

After the review of our 50-year-old marriage, Carol summed it up this way: "Time flies fastest on happy wings."

APPENDIX 5
NOTES

INTRODUCTION

1. Miller, Susan (2019). "37 years ago: The horror and heroism of Air Florida Flight 90." *USA Today*. Jan 13: https://www.usatoday.com/story/news/nation/2019/01/13/air-florida-flight-90-crashed-potomac-37-years-ago/2565245002/

2. Bacchus, Al & Carol (1999). *Personal Wellness: How to Go the Distance*. meduwell.com publishing.

3. Staff (2020). "Concept of Archetypes by Carl Jung." Carl Jung Resources: https://www.carl-jung.net/

4. Moore, Robert and Gillette, Douglas (1990). *King, Warrior, Magician and Lover: Rediscovering the Archetypes of the Mature Masculine*. HarperCollins.

5. Zhan, Yan, *et al.* (2015). "Differences between Male and Female Consumers of Complementary and Alternative Medicine in a National US Population: A Secondary Analysis of 2012 NIHS Data." *Evidence-Based Complementary and Alternative Medicine*, vol. 2015, Article ID 413173, https://doi.org/10.1155/2015/413173

CHAPTER 1: SELF, LOVE, AND OTHERS

1. Lewis, C. S (1960). *The Four Loves*. Harcourt Brace & Co.

   Other writers, seminar leaders and therapists expanded the list of Greek words for love to seven. (See: https://www.psychologytoday.

com/us/blog/hide-and-seek/201606/these-are-the-7-types-love)
The additional words seem to add some meaning to therapy, but I prefer the classic four for understanding love.

2. Baker, Shirley A. PhD (1990) "Socratic Method for Teaching Problem Solving," *Journal of Health Occupations Education*: 5 (2) Article 7.

3. Bacchus, Al & Carol (1999). *Personal Wellness: How to Go the Distance.* meduwell.com publishing.

CHAPTER 2: WHOLE-PERSON LOVE

1. Fortenberry, J. Dennis (2013). "Puberty and Adolescent Sexuality." *Hormones and Behavior,* Jul, 64(2): 280-287.

2. FDA News Release (2019). FDA approves new treatment for hypoactive sexual desire disorder in premenopausal women. https://www.fda.gov/news-events/press-announcements/ fda-approves-new-treatment-hypoactive-sexual-desir e-disorder-premenopausal-women

3. Helminiak, Daniel A. (2006). "Sex as a Spiritual Exercise." Sex and the Church, *Reflections.* Yale Divinity School: https://reflections.yale.edu/ article/sex-and-church/sex-spiritual-exercise.

4. Harvard Men's Health (2019). "Is sex exercise? And is it hard on the heart?" Retrieved August, 2020 from: https://www.health.harvard.edu/ mens-health/is-sex-exercise-and-is-it-hard-on-the-heart

5. Shakespeare, William (1602). *Twelfth Night, or, What You Will.* http:// shakespeare.mit.edu/twelfth_night/full.html

6. Gere, Cathy (2017). *Pleasure, Pain and the Greater Good.* The University of Chicago Press.

7. Winch, Guy (2018). *How to Fix a Broken Heart.* Simon & Schuster.

8. Berscheid, PhD, Ellen (2010). Love in the Fourth Dimension. *Annual Review of Psychology, 61:*1-25.

9. Finkel, Eli J. (2017). "The Psychology of Close Relationships: Fourteen Core Principles." *Annual Review of Psychology, 68:*383-411.

10. Ormel, J., VonKorff, M., Jeronimus, B. F., & Riese, H. (2017). "Set-Point Theory and personality development: Reconciliation

of a paradox." In J. Specht (Ed.), Personality development across the lifespan (p. 117–137). Elsevier Academic Press. https://doi.org/10.1016/B978-0-12-804674-6.00009-0

11. Waldinger, Robert J, and Schulz, Marc S. (2010). "What's Love Got to Do with It? Social Functioning, Perceived Health, and Daily Happiness in Married Octogenarians." *Psychol Aging*, 25(2): 422-431. Retrieved Aug 15, 2020 from https://www.ncbi.nlm.nih.gov/pmc/articles/PMC2896234/

12. Sorensen, James, *et al* (2018). "Evaluation and Treatment of Female Sexual Pain: A Clinical Review. *Cureus*: 10(3) doi: 10.7759/cureus.2379.

CHAPTER 3: HEALTHCARE—FROM PSEUDOSCIENCE TO WELLNESS

1. Ackernecht, Erwin (1982). *A Short History of Medicine*. Johns Hopkins University Press.

2. Purdue University Lecture Notes (2020). *History of Chemistry*. Retrieved August, 2020 from http://chemed.chem.purdue.edu/genchem/history/dalton.html

3. Flexner, A. (1910). *Medical Education in the United States and Canada: A Report of the Carnegie Foundation for the Advancement of Teaching*. Bulletin 4.

4. Herrmann-Lingen, Christoph (2017). "The American Psychosomatic Society – integrating mind, brain, body and social context in medicine since 1942." *Biopsychosoc Med*. 11: 11. Published online 2017 Apr 8. doi: 10.1186/s13030-017-0096-6

5. Engel, George (1977). "The Need for a New Model: A Challenge to Biomedcine." *Science,* 196(4286): 129-136.

6. See the webpage for the Foundation of Alternative and Integrative Medicine, for explanation of the American Holistic Medical Association. https://www.faim.org/american-holistic-medical-association-ahma

7. Eisenberg, David, et al (1993). "Unconventional Medicine in the United States: prevalence, costs and patterns of us." *New England Journal of Medicine,* 328(4):246-252.

8. Staff (2020). "Healthy People 2030 Framework." *Office of Disease Prevention and Health Promotion. US Department of Health and Human Service.* https://www.healthypeople.gov/2020/About-Healthy-People/Development-Healthy-People-2030/Framework.

9. The Office of Care and Civility at the Health Science Center of the University of North Texas illustrates the use of the Wellness Model. https://www.unthsc.edu/care-and-civility/wellness-model/

CHAPTER 4: THE PERSONAL PURSUIT OF HAPPINESS

1. The Editors of Encyclopaedia Britannica (2018). "Declaration of the Rights of Man and of the Citizen." https://www.britannica.com/topic/Declaration-of-the-Rights-of-Man-and-of-the-Citizen.

2. Strauss, Valerie (2020). "Are Our Rights 'inalienable' or 'unalienable'?" *The Washington Post Online:* https://www.washingtonpost.com/news/answer-sheet/wp/2015/07/04/are-our-rights-inalienable-or-unalienable/

3. Editors, Emory Report (2018). "What the Declaration of Independence really means by 'pursuit of happiness'." Emory Report, July 3, 2018. https://news.emory.edu/stories/2014/06/er_pursuit_of_happiness/campus.html

4. Diener, E., Emmons, R. A., Larsen, R. J., & Griffin, S. (1985). "The Satisfaction with Life Scale." Journal of Personality Assessment, 49, 71-75.)

5. Setton, Mark K. (2020). The Pursuit of Happiness: Bringing the Science of Happiness to Life." https://www.pursuit-of-happiness.org/history-of-happiness/ed-diener/

6. Rouner, Leroy S., ed (1995). *In Pursuit of Happiness*. University of Notre Dame Press.

7. Hudson, Deal W. (1996). Happiness and the Limits of Satisfaction. Rowman & Littlefield Publishers, Inc.

8. Myers, David G. (1993). *The Pursuit of Happiness: Who Is Happy, And Why*. Harper Paperbacks.

9. Hathaway, Bill (2020). YaleNews: March 25. https://
    news.yale.edu/2020/03/25/housebound-world-finds-solac
    e-yales-science-well-being-course

10. Online Course (2020). "A Life of Happiness and Fulfillment." https://
    www.coursera.org/instructor/raghunathan

11. Lambert, Craig (2007). "The Science of Happiness." *Harvard
    Magazine*: Jan-Feb. https://harvardmagazine.com/2007/01/
    the-science-of-happiness.html

12. Tal Ben-Shahar. Speaking Matters. https://www.speakingmatters.org/
    tal-ben-shahar/

13. Handwerker, Haim (2006). "Happy Hour." *HAARETZ*, Oct 5.
    https://www.haaretz.com/1.4905342

14. Brooks, Arthur C. (2020). "How to Build a Life." *The Atlantic*. April 9.

15. Research in Positive Psychology is providing many useful tools
    and assessments to help the general public explore strategies for
    personal growth. One such resource is the Authentic Happiness
    website sponsored by the Positive Psychology Center, University of
    Pennsylvania. The director of the center is Dr. Martin E. P. Seligman.
    https://www.authentichappiness.sas.upenn.edu/home.

16. Vaillant, George E. (2012). *Triumphs of Experience—The Men of the
    Harvard Grant Study.* Harvard University Press.

17. Laboratory of Adult Development at Massachusetts General Hospital.
    https://www.massgeneral.org/psychiatry/research/laboratory-o
    f-adult-development.

18. Staff (2020). International Day of Happiness, 20 March. United
    Nations: https://www.un.org/en/observances/happiness-day

19. Pew Research Center (2019). "Religion's Relationship to
    Happiness, Civic Engagement and Health Around the World."
    Religion and Public Life, Jan 31: https://www.pewforum.
    org/2019/01/31/religions-relationship-to-happiness-civic-
    engagement-and-health-around-the-world/

20. Helliwell, John F., Richard Layard, Jeffrey Sachs, and Jan-Emmanuel De
    Neve, eds (2020). *World Happiness Report 2020.* New York: Sustainable
    Development Solutions Network: https://worldhappiness.report/

21. Blanchflower, David G. (2021). "Is happiness U-shaped everywhere? Age and subjective well-being in 145 countries." *Journal of Population Economics*, 34, 575–624. https://doi.org/10.1007/s00148-020-00797-z

CHAPTER 5: WATER FOR BODY AND SOUL

1. There are many physiology textbooks I can cite as the sources for information on water in the human body, but I prefer to give the US Geological Survey as the citation here as it has good scientific information, and a lot more – everything you can want to know about water. https://www.usgs.gov/special-topic/water-science-school/science/water-you-water-and-human-body?qt-science_center_objects=0#qt-science_center_objects

2. The National Science Foundation is a good resource for science information and the application of science in the environment. So you get sound information on the chemistry of water, and much more. The Chemistry of Water: https://www.nsf.gov/news/special_reports/water/index_low.jsp?id=properties

3. Institute of Medicine (2005). "Dietary Reference Intakes for Water, Potassium, Sodium, Chloride, and Sulfate." *The National Academies Press.* https://doi.org/10.17226/10925.

4. Perrier, Erica T. *et al* (2016). "Urine colour changes as an indicator of change in daily water intake: a quantitative analysis." Eur J Nutr., 55: 1943-1949. https://www.ncbi.nlm.nih.gov/pmc/articles/PMC4949298/

5. World Health Organization (2019). *Fact Sheet*: "Drinking Water," June 14. https://www.who.int/news-room/fact-sheets/detail/drinking-water

6. Hackett, Conrad and McClendon, David (2017). "Christians remain world's largest religious group, but they are declining in Europe." *FactTank,* April 5. Pew Research Center. https://www.pewresearch.org/fact-tank/2017/04/05/christians-remain-worlds-largest-religious-group-but-they-are-declining-in-europe/

7. Jayadev, Yashoda (2018). "Religion and Water – The Most Sacred Relationship." *Religion World.* https://www.

religionworld.in/religion-water-sacred-relationship-hinudism-is
lam-christianity-buddhism-parsi/

8. Russell, Bertrand (1956). "How to Grow Old." *Portraits from Memory and Other Essays.* Simon and Schuster.

Chapter 6: DNA for Body and Soul

1. Staff (2020). "What Is DNA?" *Genetics Home Reference.* https://ghr. nlm.nih.gov/primer/basics/dna

2. Staff (2020). "About Genomics." *National Human Genome Research Institute.* https://www.genome.gov/about-genomics

3. Khan, Suliman, *et al.* (2016). "Role of Recombinant DNA Technology to Improve Life." *Int J Genomics*, 2405954. Published online 2016 Dec 8. doi: 10.1155/2016/2405954

4. Staff (2020). "Genetic Disorders." *National Human Genome Research Institute.* https://www.genome.gov/For-Patients-and-Families/ Genetic-Disorders.

5. Staff (2017). "Antioxidants and Cancer Prevention." *National Cancer Institute.* https://www.cancer.gov/about-cancer/causes-prevention/risk/ diet/antioxidants-fact-sheet.

6. Staff (2019). "Using Dietary Supplements Wisely." *National Center for Complementary and Integrative Medicine.* https://www.nccih.nih.gov/ health/using-dietary-supplements-wisely.

7. Knight, J. A. (2000). "Review: Free Radicals, Antioxidants, and the Immune System.) *Ann Clin Lab Sci* Apr;30(2):145-58.

Chapter 7: Energy and Oxygen for Body and Soul

1. Staff (2016). "Our Energy Sources: The Sun." *National Academy of Sciences*: http://needtoknow.nas.edu/energy/energy-sources/the-sun/

2. Cain Fraser (2015). "How does the sun produce energy?" *Science X:* Physorg.com https://phys.org/news/2015-12-sun-energy.html.

3. Staff (2020). "The Earth-Atmosphere Energy Balance." *National Oceanic and Atmospheric Administration*: https://www.weather.gov/jetstream/energy

4. OpenStax (2016). *Concepts of Biology*. Rice University: Creative Commons Attribution 4.0 International License. http://cnx.org/content/col11487/latest/

   One of the greatest gifts of technology to college students currently is free science textbooks online, which may otherwise cost upwards of $200 US. For further reading on Photosynthesis and Cellular Respiration, see relevant chapters in the online textbook above. I currently use that in teaching the online course "Introduction to Biology" at University of Maryland Global Campus, and highly recommend it.

5. Staff (2020). "Body Weight Planner: Balancing Your Food and Activity." National Institute of Diabetes, Digestive and Kidney Disease https://www.niddk.nih.gov/bwp

6. Mead, Nathaniel M (2008). "Benefits of Sunlight: A Bright Spot for Human Health." *Environ Health Perspect*. Apr 116(4), A160-A167. https://www.ncbi.nlm.nih.gov/pmc/articles/PMC2290997/

7. Staff (2019). "Ultraviolet (UV) Radiation." American Cancer Society. https://www.cancer.org/cancer/cancer-causes/radiation-exposure/uv-radiation.html

8. Staff (2020). "Relaxation Techniques: Breath control helps quell errant stress response." *Harvard Health Publishing*: https://www.health.harvard.edu/mind-and-mood/relaxation-techniques-breath-control-helps-quell-errant-stress-response

CHAPTER 8: NUTRITION FOR BODY AND SOUL

1. Dietary Guidelines Advisory Committee (2020). "*Scientific Report of the 2020 Dietary Guidelines Advisory Committee: Advisory Report to the Secretary of Agriculture and the Secretary of Health and Human Services." U.S. Department of Agriculture, Agricultural Research Service, Washington, DC.* https://www.dietaryguidelines.gov/2020-advisory-committee-report

2. Buettner, Dan and Skemp, Sam (2016). "Blue Zones: Lessons from the World's Longest Lived." *Am J Lifestyle Med*. 2016 Sep-Oct; 10(5):

318–321. doi: 10.1177/1559827616637066. https://www.ncbi.nlm.
nih.gov/pmc/articles/PMC6125071/

3. Worrall, Simon (2015). "Here Are the Secrets to a Long and Healthy
    Life." *National Geographic, April 12.* https://www.nationalgeographic.
    com/news/2015/04/150412-longevity-health-blue-zones-obesity-
    diet-ngbooktalk/#close

4. Staff (2017). "Paleo Diet: what is it and why is it so popular?"
    Mayo Clinic, Aug 8. https://www.mayoclinic.org/healthy-lifestyle/
    nutrition-and-healthy-eating/in-depth/paleo-diet/art-20111182

5. Shilpa, J. and Mohan V. (2018). "Ketogenic Diets: Boon or bane?"
    Indian J Med Res. 2018 Sep; 148(3): 251–253. doi: 10.4103/ijmr.
    IJMR_1666_18
    https://www.ncbi.nlm.nih.gov/pmc/articles/PMC6251269/

6. Klok, M. D. *et al* (2006). "The role of leptin and ghrelin in the
    regulation of food intake and body weight in humans: a review."
    Wiley Online Library, Aug 24: https://onlinelibrary.wiley.com/doi/
    full/10.1111/j.1467-789X.2006.00270.x.

7. Staff (2014). "What is Mindfulness?" *Mindful Health and Safety, Univ
    of Cal., Irvine:* https://sites.uci.edu/mindfulhs/what-is-mindfulness/

8. Staff (2016). "8 steps to mindful eating." *Harvard Health Publishing*,
    Jan: https://www.health.harvard.edu/staying-healthy/8-step
    s-to-mindful-eating

9. Nelson, Joseph B. (2017). "Mindful Eating: The Art of Presence
    While You Eat." *Diabetes Spectr.* Aug; 30(3): 171–174. doi: 10.2337/
    ds17-0015
    https://www.ncbi.nlm.nih.gov/pmc/articles/PMC5556586/

Chapter 9: Stress Adaptation for Body and Soul

1. Siang Yong Tan and A Yip (2018). "Hans Selye (1907 – 1982):
    Founder of the stress theory." *Singapore Med J.* Apr; 59(4): 170–171.
    doi: 10.11622/smedj.2018043, https://www.ncbi.nlm.nih.gov/pmc/
    articles/PMC5915631/

2. Selye, H. (1979). *Stress of My Life: A Scientist's Memoirs*. Van Nostrand
    Reinhold Company.

3. A video of Dr. Herbert Benson leading a 5-minute practice of the relaxation response can be viewed on the website for the Benson-Henry Institute for Mind Body Medicine at Massachusetts General Hospital. https://bensonhenryinstitute.org/about-us-dr-herbert-benson/

4. Selye H. (1956). *The Stress of Life*. McGraw-Hill Book Company.

5. Selye H. (1976). "The stress concept." *Can. Med. Assoc. J. 115:718.*

6. Godoy, Livea Dornela, *et al* (2018). "A Comprehensive Overview on Stress Neurobiology: Basic Concepts and Clinical Implications." *Front Behav Neurosci.* Jul 3; 12: 127. doi: 10.3389/fnbeh.2018.00127. https://www.ncbi.nlm.nih.gov/pmc/articles/PMC6043787/

7. Staff (2020). "Understanding the stress response." *Harvard Health Publishing*, July 6. https://www.health.harvard.edu/staying-healthy/understanding-the-stress-response.

8. Staff (2019). "Chronic stress puts your health at risk." *Mayo Clinic*, March 19. https://www.mayoclinic.org/healthy-lifestyle/stress-management/in-depth/stress/art-20046037

9. Staff (2019). "Stress symptoms: Effects on your body and behavior." *Mayo Clinic,* April 4. https://www.mayoclinic.org/healthy-lifestyle/stress-management/in-depth/stress/art-20046037

10. Naidoo, MD, Uma (2019). "Nutritional strategies to ease anxiety." *Harvard Health Publishing*, August 20: https://www.health.harvard.edu/blog/nutritional-strategies-to-ease-anxiety-201604139441

11. Li, Ye, *et al* (2017). "Dietary patterns and depression risks: A meta-analysis." *Psychiatry Res.*, July: 253:373-382. doi: 10.1016/j.psychres.2017.04.020. https://pubmed.ncbi.nlm.nih.gov/28431261/

12. Staff (2020). "Exercising to relax." Harvard Health Publishing, July 7. https://www.health.harvard.edu/staying-healthy/exercising-to-relax

CHAPTER 10: WORK AND REST FOR BODY AND SOUL

1. The Advisory Committee (2018). "Second Edition of the Physical Activity Guidelines for Americans." *President's Council on Sports,*

Fitness and Nutrition, USDHHS. https://www.hhs.gov/fitness/be-active/physical-activity-guidelines-for-americans/index.html

2. Staff (2020). "Benefits of Physical Activity." *Centers for Disease Control and Prevention*, Aug 11. https://www.cdc.gov/physicalactivity/basics/pa-health/index.htm.

3. Staff (2020). "Healthy Weight: Finding a Balance." *Centers for Disease Control and Prevention*, Aug 17: https://www.cdc.gov/healthyweight/calories/index.html

4. Staff (2020). "Healthy Weight: Assessing Your Weight." *Centers for Disease Control and Prevention,* July 1: https://www.cdc.gov/healthyweight/assessing/index.html

5. Staff (2020). "Physical Activity: Target Heart Rate and Estimated Maximum Heart Rate." *Centers for Disease Control and Prevention*, April 10: https://www.cdc.gov/physicalactivity/basics/measuring/heartrate.htm

6. Staff (2018). "Rethinking the 30-minute workout." *Harvard Health Publishing,* Sept: https://www.health.harvard.edu/staying-healthy/rethinking-the-30-minute-workout.

7. Mull, Amanda (2019). "What 10,000 Steps Will Really Get You." *The Atlantic*, May 31: https://www.theatlantic.com/health/archive/2019/05/10000-steps-rule/590785/

8. The "Move Your Way" program has several online tools, and links to reliable information on activities for all ages. A starting point for this helpful plan can be accessed at https://health.gov/moveyourway.

9. Elson, L. E. ed (2018). "Stretching: 35 Exercises to Improve Flexibility and Reduce Pain." *Harvard Health Publishing*: https://www.health.harvard.edu/exercise-and-fitness/stretching-35-exercises-to-improve-flexibility-and-reduce-pain

10. Jiang, Kevin (2020). "Fruit fly study reveals gut's role in causing death by sleep deprivation." *Harvard Gazette*, June 4: https://news.harvard.edu/gazette/story/2020/06/study-reveals-guts-role-in-causing-death-by-sleep-deprivation/

11. Staff (2020). "Sleep Deprivation and Deficiency." *National Heart, Lung and Blood Institute.* https://www.nhlbi.nih.gov/health-topics/sleep-deprivation-and-deficiency

12. Wein, Harrison, ed (2013). "The Benefits of Slumber: Why You Need a Good Night's Sleep." *NIH News in Health*, April: https://newsinhealth.nih.gov/2013/04/benefits-slumber

13. General Services Administration (2019). "Federal Management Regulation (FMR); Sleeping in Federal Buildings." *Federal Register*, Nov 5: https://www.federalregister.gov/documents/2019/11/05/2019-24102/federal-management-regulation-fmr-sleeping-in-federal-buildings.

14. Staff (2014). "Key Sleep Disorders." *Centers for Disease Control and Prevention,* Dec 10: https://www.cdc.gov/sleep/about_sleep/key_disorders.html

CHAPTER 11: GROWTH AND REPRODUCTION FOR BODY AND SOUL

1. Betts, J. Gordon, *et al*, eds. (2013). *Anatomy and Physiology*. OpenStax: https://opentextbc.ca/anatomyandphysiology/chapter/27-2-anatomy-and-physiology-of-the-female-reproductive-system/

2. Spielman, Rose M, *et al.* (2019). *Psychology*. OpenStax: https://openstax.org/books/psychology/pages/9-1-what-is-lifespan-development

3. Nelson, Charles A. *et al* (2014). *Romania's Abandoned Children: Deprivation, Brain Development, and the Struggle for Recovery*. Harvard University Press.

4. Blight, Alysse (2019). "The Shettles Method of Sex Selection." *The Embryo Project Encyclopedia*, Arizona State University: https://embryo.asu.edu/pages/shettles-method-sex-selection

CHAPTER 12: YOUR INNER WARRIOR, MIRACLE-WORKER, LOVER, AND RULER

1. Wangler, Joan Patricia, MCC, MA, Program Faculty. Center for Excellence in Public Leadership, The George Washington University, 2020: https://leadershipcoaching.cepl.gwu.edu/our-team/program-faculty/joan-patricia-wangler/

2. Moore, Robert and Gillette, Douglas (1990). *King, Warrior, Magician and Lover: Rediscovering the Archetypes of the Mature Masculine*. HarperCollins.

3. Bacchus, Alban (2005). "The Gaius Principle: A Christ-centered approach to health." *Adventist Review*, 1512: https://www. adventistreview.org/archives/2005-1512/story3.html

4. Gladwell, Malcolm (2002). *The Tipping Point: How Little Things Can Make a Big Difference.* Little, Brown and Company.

5. Bacchus, Al (2003). "Let's Start a Wellness Epidemic." *Adventist Review*, 1506: https://www.adventistreview.org/archives/2003-1506/story1.html

6. Bacchus, Al (2006). "10 Health Principles for Body and Soul." *Adventist Review*, 1532-8: https://www.adventistreview.org/2006-1532-8

7. Center for Spirituality, Theology and Health. Duke Center for Aging and Human Development, Duke University: https:// spiritualityandhealth.duke.edu/index.php

8. Kaufman, Scott Barry (2019). "The Light Triad vs. Dark Triad of Personality." Scientific American, March 19: https://blogs. scientificamerican.com/beautiful-minds/the-light-triad-vs-dark-triad-of-personality/

9. Kaufman, Scott Barry. https://scottbarrykaufman.com/

10. Thoreau, Henry D. (1854). *Walden: Life in the Woods.* Tickner and Fields. Internet Archive Online Library: https://archive.org/details/ waldenorlifeinwo1854thor/page/n3/mode/2up

11. Plapp, Fred (2020). "The COVID-19 Pandemic: A Summary." *The Pathologist Subspecialties*, July 6: https://thepathologist.com/ subspecialties/the-covid-19-pandemic-a-summary

12. United Nations (2020). "World Economic Situation and Prospects as of mid-2020." *Department of Economics and Social Affairs,* May 13: https://www.un.org/development/desa/dpad/publication/ world-economic-situation-and-prospects-as-of-mid-2020/

    "The projected cumulative output losses during 2020 and 2021—nearly $8.5 trillion—will wipe out nearly all output gains of the previous four years."

13. Losavio, Joseph (2020). "George Floyd: these are the injustices that led to protests in the United States." *World Economic Forum*, June 5: https://www.weforum.org/agenda/2020/06/this-is-what-has-led-to-george-floyd-protests-in-the-united-states/

14. Biography.com, eds (2020). "John Lewis Biography." *Biography. com Website*, July 18: https://www.biography.com/political-figure/ john-lewis.

15. Georgetown Law (2020). "A Timeline of the Legalization of Same Sex Marriage in the U. S." *Georgetown Law Library*, July 29: https:// guides.ll.georgetown.edu/c.php?g=592919&p=4182201

16. UN News (2020). "US Supreme Court ruling 'extremely positive' for LGBT community, says UN Rights Expert." Global Perspectives, June 17: https://news.un.org/en/story/2020/06/1066482

17. Cameron, PhD, Elizabeth E. *et al*, (2019). Global Health Security Index. GHS Index.org: https://www.ghsindex.org/.

18. Staff (2020). "Statistics and Research Coronavirus Pandemic: What is the global situation now?" *Our World in Data*: Aug 22: https:// ourworldindata.org/coronavirus

19. Boushey, Heather and Park, Somin (2020). "The coronavirus recession and economic inequality: A roadmap to recovery and long-term structural change." *Washington Center for Equitable Growth*, Aug 7: https://equitablegrowth.org/the-coronavirus-recession-an d-economic-inequality-a-roadmap-to-recovery-and-long-ter m-structural-change/

CHAPTER 13: YOUR BOOK ON LOVE, WELLNESS, AND HAPPINESS

1. The C. Everett Koop Institute at Dartmouth. https://sites.dartmouth. edu/koop/c-everett-koop/

2. Frankl, Viktor E. (1959). *Man's Search for Meaning*. Beacon Press: https://www.amazon.com/Mans-Search-Meaning-Viktor-Frankl/ dp/080701429X#reader_080701429X

3. Bacchus, Al and Carol (1999). *Personal Wellness: How to Go the Distance*. Meduwell.com publishing: https://www.amazon.com/ Personal-Wellness-How-Go-Distance/dp/0967483409/ref=sr_1_2? dchild=1&keywords=personal+wellness%3A+how+to+go+the+dist ance&qid=1595851068&s=books&sr=1-2 (When this is no longer displayed on Amazon, it will be found on the author's website, www. albanbacchus.com)

4. The Robert M. Berne Cardiovascular Research Center. University of Virginia, Charlottesville: https://www.cvrc.virginia.edu/

5. BIOLOGOS: https://biologos.org/about-us

6. Tan, Shelly, et al (2021). "How one of America's ugliest days unraveled inside and outside the Capitol." *The Washington Post*, Jan 9.

7. Lawton, Kim (2004). "John Lewis – Extended Interview." PBS: Religion and Ethics Newsweekly, Jan 16: https://www.pbs. org/wnet/religionandethics/2004/01/16/january-16-2004-joh n-lewis-extended-interview/2897/

8. Gandhi, M. K. (2002). "My Life is My Message. What Is Satyagraha?" *Gandhi Book Centre*: https://www.mkgandhi.org/faq/q17.htm

9. Lewis, John (2020). "Together, You Can Redeem the Soul of Our Nation." *The New York Times*, July 30: https://www.nytimes. com/2020/07/30/opinion/john-lewis-civil-rights-america. html?utm_source=pocket-newtab

CHAPTER 14: FINAL REFLECTIONS ON LOVE, WELLNESS, AND HAPPINESS

1. For all passages of Scripture used in this manuscript, I accessed the study helps provided on the Internet, especially from the site "*Blue Letter Bible*," https://www.blueletterbible.org/

2. Huffman, MD, Jeff C. (2019). "Optimism and Health." *JAMA Network*, Sept 27: https://jamanetwork.com/journals/ jamanetworkopen/fullarticle/2752094

3. Bacchus, PhD, Al (2006). "10 Health Principles for Body and Soul." *Adventist Review,* Nov 9: https://www.adventistreview.org/2006-1532-8

4. Gladwell, Malcolm (2002). *The Tipping Point: How Little Things Can Make a Big Difference.* Little, Brown and Company.

5. Bacchus, Al (2003). "Let's Start a Wellness Epidemic." *Adventist Review*, 1506. https://www.adventistreview.org/archives/2003-1506/story1.html

6. Whitmore, Sir John (2017). *Coaching for Performance: The Principles and Practice of Coaching and Leadership.* Nicholas Brealey Publishing.

ACKNOWLEDGMENTS

I gratefully acknowledge the contributions of the following amazing friends and colleagues for their assistance and critique to make this a more enjoyable read than it would be without their help.

- o Rick Bacchus for his detailed reading and suggestions on my second draft
- o Harold Grosboll for his suggestions on the Note to the Reader among other constructive critique
- o My editor, Felicity Fox, for the extensive edits which were needed to add clarity and conciseness to my long, complicated sentences
- o My proof-reader, Kaitlyn Madsen, who not only caught the typos and punctuation mistakes but also offered edits that added clarity to what I was trying to say
- o My beta readers: Eugene Kitney, Reuel Bacchus, Lenroy Thomas, Tom Benner, Syletha Clark, and Stephen Walwyn
- o Dr. Tony Colson for his encouragement, helpful coaching, and writing a Foreword.

Your critique and encouragement contributed greatly to my effort to complete this work. Your practical support of my vision means a lot. I treasure our friendship and continued association.

Greatest gratitude is reserved for my wife, Carol, who is my alpha reader for everything I have written since 1970, and my co-visionary for a life of love, wellness, and happiness. Thanks for always offering objective critique to all my new ideas, even allowing me the freedom to fail without any condemnation. I love you.

ABOUT THE AUTHOR

Al Bacchus is promoting Christ-Centered Wellness. As a writer, coach, retired college professor and speaker, he helps individuals and Christian organizations to structure their health promotion activities with a goal to generate growth towards maturity in Christ.

Dr. Bacchus grew up on the Caribbean Island of St. Vincent. His college and graduate education were in the USA. He earned his BS and MA degrees from Andrews University, and his PhD in human physiology from Michigan State University.

His growth to differentiate between religion and spirituality began as a teaching assistant in the Department of Health Education at the University of Maryland. Here, he developed and taught the course "Personal Wellness & Self-Realization." He used the framework for that course to develop and teach "Christ-Centered Wellness," at Washington Adventist University.

As he approaches his 75th birthday, he finds great joy in sharing his outlook on how to blend science, religion, and psychology to ensure the outcome of happiness.

A brief perusal of his life review (Chapter 13), and his OPUS (Chapter 14), will fill out the picture of the intellectual and practical struggles that led to his writing *Love, Wellness, and Happiness.*

He is happy as he plans for his remaining years of life. He lives in Martinsburg, West Virginia, with his wife of 50 years. They have three children and four grandchildren.

www.albanbacchus.com

Free Online Course!

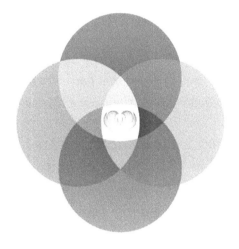

"Love and Christ-Centered Wellness"

In this 7-session discussion, Dr. Bacchus shares his vision for challenging Christians to grow to maturity in Christ.

See schedule at:
www.albanbacchus.com

This Book Supports School Building Projects Worldwide

50% of the profits from this book are donated to building schools where the need exists worldwide.

The first project is the elementary school from which I graduated in 1959. It started in the home of a relative in the village of Richland Park, St. Vincent. *In its 75 years of existence, it has never had a building to call its own.*

More details, pictures, and progress reports can be found at www.albanbacchus.com.

Each new building project will be announced and publicized via the website above. If you have a school building project being planned, contact us to discuss how we may support you via this ongoing program.

Research

Proceeds from sales of this book will support structured research on the effects of a 7-week protocol of Christ-Centered Wellness compared to any other wellness promotion protocol.

Challenge to any Christian College, University, or Church
If chapters 12–14 of this book inspire you to conduct your wellness promotion program with data collection worthy of publication, I will partner with you to fund the effort.

Together, we will find resources to:
o Sponsor your qualified research director to attend the Duke Research Workshop described here: https://spiritualityandhealth.duke.edu/index.php/5-day-summer-research-course

o Support the research project from concept to publication.

For more details and to apply for this sponsorship, please see Research at:

www.albanbacchus.com

Explore Your Spiritual DNA with Dr. Tony Colson

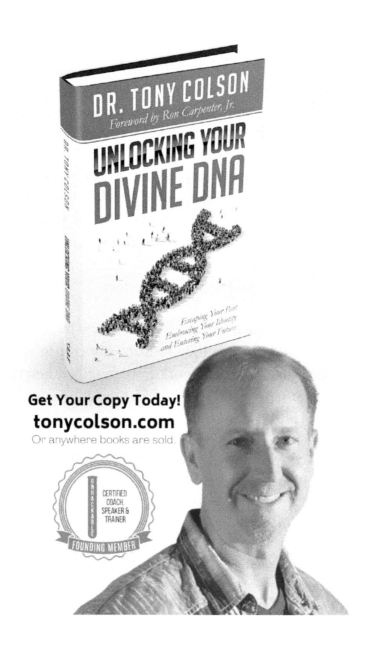

Get Your Copy Today!
tonycolson.com
Or anywhere books are sold.

Lightning Source UK Ltd.
Milton Keynes UK
UKHW020355100821
388593UK00009B/724/J

9 781647 467661